Delivering Citizenship

Bertelsmann Stiftung, European Policy Centre,
Migration Policy Institute (eds.)

Delivering Citizenship

The Transatlantic Council on Migration

| Verlag Bertelsmann**Stiftung**

Bibliographic information published by the Deutsche Nationalbibliothek

The Deutsche Nationalbibliothek lists this publication in the
Deutsche Nationalbibliografie; detailed bibliographic data
is available on the Internet at http://dnb.d-nb.de.

© 2008 Verlag Bertelsmann Stiftung, Gütersloh
Responsible: Christal Morehouse
Production editor: Christiane Raffel
Cover design: Nadine Humann
Cover illustration: mauritius images/Photoshot
Typesetting: Katrin Berkenkamp, Designwerkstatt 12, Bielefeld
Printing: Hans Kock Buch- und Offsetdruck GmbH, Bielefeld
ISBN 978-3-86793-027-7

www.bertelsmann-stiftung.org/publications

Contents

Part III: Summary of the Discussion

Foreword

The magnitude, effects and rapidly shifting patterns of international migration have never been more pronounced, widely felt or far-reaching than they are today—shaping the issue into a major element for policymakers on both sides of the Atlantic.

The complexity of the issue has increased exponentially since the Iron Curtain was torn open almost two decades ago. What has emerged is an "Age of Mobility" that is affecting most countries, certainly those in the transatlantic sphere. Diversity in society has become a new status quo in many countries which had not experienced significant immigration previously. Balancing the requirements for economic growth, social justice, cohesion and national security in a context of sweeping economic, demographic and technological change has become a top priority for governments as well as for public and private actors. Against such a backdrop of dynamic and fast-moving change, societies and governments are struggling to respond coherently and to positively manage the consequent social change. It is clear that policy responses to the challenges and opportunities of growing global mobility are running far behind the impact of migration, both real and imagined. And public skepticism about the value of most immigration and about the ability of governments to manage it well appears to be higher than at any time in recent memory—further complicating policymakers' task.

The Transatlantic Council on Migration has been created to fill gaps that are apparent in the body of knowledge available to policymakers. The expertise that its distinguished members bring to the table is complemented by the broad knowledge and experience of the many transatlantic institutions that have united in supporting its work.

Delivering cutting-edge policy recommendations is a key part of the Council's work. Therefore, the Migration Policy Institute (MPI) in Washington, DC and its policy partners—the Bertelsmann Stiftung and the European Policy Centre (in cooperation with the King Baudouin Foundation)—are pleased to present you with the first in a series of Council publications. This first book focuses on advancing social cohesion and social justice through more coherent citizenship and integration policies. This volume will inform interested readers about the main policy challenges that European and North American countries face. It proposes a number of enlightened policy options in response to these challenges.

The book is divided into three parts. Part One begins with an introduction, describing the structure, objectives, approach, evolution, work and long-term aims of the Council. This is followed by the Council's Statement on citizenship. The Statement distills the policy ideas which emerged during the first meeting of the Council on April 24–25, 2008 in Bellagio, Italy. Although it reflects the deliberations of the Council, final responsibility for the content of the book rests with the authors.

Part Two contains five original contributions from leading academics in North America and Europe. These in-depth analyses, commissioned expressly for the Council, provided the necessary context for discussions during the Council's meeting in April 2008.

The first chapter of Part Two, entitled "Stakeholder Citizenship: An Idea Whose Time Has Come?", was written by Rainer Bauböck (Professor and Chair of Social and Political Theory at the European University Institute in Florence). The chapter describes the political and social context in which citizenship is being discussed on both sides of the Atlantic.

The second chapter of Part Two, entitled "Dual Citizenship in an Age of Mobility", is the work of Professor Thomas Faist and Research Assistant Jürgen Gerdes, both at the University of Bielefeld. They describe how, in a globalizing world in which traditional barriers are quickly coming down, more and more people are taking on multiple, overlapping identities. This trend, coupled with the reality of increasing diversity within western societies, sits uneasily with citizenship requirements. The promotion of a single national identity competes with transnational concepts of belonging. Increasing transnationalism is influencing national debates and citizenship policies, especially in Europe. Yet more than ten countries in Europe still maintain formal restrictions on dual nationality.

The third chapter of this section, entitled "Local Voting Rights for Non-Nationals in Europe: What We Know and What We Need to Learn", was written by Kees Groenendijk, (Professor at the Center for Migration Law at Radboud University, Nijmegen). Professor Groenendijk examines what is essentially a pre-citizenship debate and asks whether the granting of local voting rights increases integration and encourages citizenship acquisition.

The fourth chapter, entitled "A New Citizenship Bargain for the Age of Mobility? Citizenship Requirements in Europe and North America", was written by Randall Hansen (Associate Professor and Holder of the Canada Research Chair at the Department of Political Science, University of Toronto). He examines the trend, especially in European states, for governments to adopt a range of measures in response to migration that are aimed at revitalizing the sense of national identity and national citizenship. Such moves have often been controversial. Professor Hansen examines evidence to find out which of the various measures work well and which do not, and the reasons why.

The final chapter of Part Two, entitled "The Complexities of Immigration Politics and Policies", was written by Jennifer Hochschild (Henry LaBarre Jayne Professor of Government, Harvard University) and John Mollenkopf (Distinguished Professor of Political Science and Sociology, CUNY Graduate Center). This chapter considers the debate about migration in a broader perspective of public opinion and the politics of immigration.

Part Three of the book is a summary of the discussion at the Council's meeting in April 2008. It provides readers with a record of the deliberations of the Council members and experts who took part. It is written in accordance with the Chatham House Rule of not revealing the identities of the various speakers, a rule intended to aid free and uninhibited discussion. Part Three also contains biographies of the Council Members and Staff.

We hope that this book will stimulate increased transatlantic exchange and dialogue on issues of citizenship and inclusion. The Migration Policy Institute in Washington (DC) and its policy partners (the Bertelsmann Stiftung and the European Policy Centre) look forward, in this and future volumes, to making good use of the opportunity to advance thinking about migration policy on both sides of the Atlantic.

| *Demetrios G. Papademetriou* | *Gunter Thielen* | *Hans Martens* |
| Migration Policy Institute | Bertelsmann Stiftung | European Policy Centre |

Part I: The Transatlantic Council on Migration

Introduction: The Aims of the Transatlantic Council on Migration

Transatlantic Council on Migration

The 21st century promises to be the "Age of Mobility". More and more people around the globe, from an ever greater number of backgrounds, are migrating. As Europe and North America absorb a larger and more diverse inflow, some policymakers, commentators and academics have begun to question whether their societies can cope with the influx.

Citizenship has emerged as one of the key policy battlegrounds for such concerns. Citizenship lies at an intersection of a host of social policy issues because it provides definitions of identity, belonging and, perhaps above all, participation in key aspects of society, such as voting.

Governments are rushing to catch up with public anxieties, typically responding with laws and regulations. The pressure to bring citizenship policy closer to immigration and integration policy has been driven by several forces, among which are:

- Growing security concerns around terrorism, with citizenship viewed as a means of providing a bulwark of values.
- Increased mobility, with migrants staying for much shorter periods of time and seeking rights in more than one country.
- Greater volume and diversity of immigration, which has led to increasing number of immigrant communities from a wider range of countries. Such communities are often perceived as being enclaves, with their own languages, and with culturally distinct markers (such as minority religions).

In light of such changes and challenges, how can we analyze citizenship policy? This book is an attempt to understand some aspects of the citizenship debate from a policy perspective through the deliberations and thinking of the Transatlantic Council on Migration. The following introduction offers an overview of the Transatlantic Council on Migration: its mission, make-up, support and operation.

The Transatlantic Council on Migration

This book is the first major product of the Transatlantic Council on Migration. The Council is a new initiative of the Migration Policy Institute (MPI) in Washington, DC. The Bertelsmann Stiftung and the European Policy Centre (in cooperation with the King Baudouin Foundation) are the Council's policy partners. The Council is supported by the Carnegie Corporation of New York, the Ford Foundation, the Rockefeller Foundation, the Hellenic Migration Policy Institute (IMEPO) and the governments of the Netherlands and Norway.

The permanent Council members are: Giuliano Amato, former Prime Minister and Minister of the Interior in Italy; Xavier Becerra, Member of the US House of Representatives since 1992 and Assistant Speaker of the House; Mel Cappe, President of the Institute of Research on Public Policy and formerly the High Commissioner to the United Kingdom; Armin Laschet, Minister for Intergenerational Affairs, Family, Women and Integration in North Rhine-Westphalia, Germany, and a former parliamentarian of the European Union; Libe Rieber-Mohn, the State Secretary for integration, immigration and diversity matters in the Norwegian Department of Labor and Inclusion; Ana Palacio, Senior Vice President for International Affairs and Marketing for AREVA, and formerly parliamentarian of the European Union, Foreign Minister of Spain, and Senior Vice President and General Counsel of the World Bank; Trevor Phillips, Chairman of the UK Commission on Equality and Human Rights; Rita Süssmuth, former President (Speaker) of the German Bundestag (1988–1998), and twice leader of Germany's Independent Commissions on

Immigration and on Integration in the first half of this decade; Antonio Vitorino, partner in the international law firm Gonçalves Pereira, Castelo Branco & Associados, and former European Union Commissioner for Justice and Home Affairs (1999–2004), and former Deputy Prime Minister of Portugal.

The Transatlantic Council is convened by Demetrios G. Papademetriou, President of the Migration Policy Institute (MPI); its Executive Director is Gregory A. Maniatis, Senior Fellow, MPI.

Mission

The Transatlantic Council on Migration is a unique deliberative body that examines vital policy issues and informs migration policymaking processes across the Atlantic community. Its approach is evidence-based, progressive yet pragmatic, and ardently independent. Council members and their guests combine exceptional political and public influence with profound interest and experience in issues related to migration.

The Council has a dual mission:

- To help inform, and thus influence, the transatlantic immigration and integration agendas by proactively identifying critical policy issues, analyzing them in light of the best research and mature judgment, wherever they exist, and bringing them to the attention of the public. In so doing, the Council's work will also build the applied, comparative, international, analytical infrastructure—a virtual and easily accessible library—that promotes better-informed policy-making on these issues.

- To serve as a resource for governments as they grapple with the challenges and opportunities associated with international migration. Council members representing governments (and other governments, as appropriate) are encouraged to bring policy initiatives to the Council so that they can be analyzed, vetted and improved before implementation—and/or evaluated after they have been executed. This activity will be carried out under the Chatham House

15

Rule. Interested supranational and intergovernmental institutions and processes (such as the Global Forum on International Migration and Development) will also benefit from the Council's work.

The Council's Approach

The Council's work is disseminated to capital cities through the initiative of Council members (supported by MPI and the project's Management Board), and to European institutions and the broader Brussels community through a policy partnership with the European Policy Centre and the Bertelsmann Stiftung.

The Council's work is at the cutting edge of policy analysis and evaluation, and is thus an essential tool of policymaking. Among the policy fields that the Council explores are: (a) advancing social cohesion and social justice through more thoughtful citizenship and integration policies; (b) enhancing economic growth and competitiveness through immigration; (c) encouraging and facilitating greater mobility through better security; and (d) understanding better the complex links between migration and development. The Council's work is informed by: a belief in adhering to the rule of law across the board; commitment to a rights-sensitive agenda rooted in fairness; and the determination that the increasing diversity that migration has brought about—covering virtually the entire advanced industrial world—can be managed smartly and to advantage.

The policy options placed before the Council for its deliberation are analyzed and vetted by some of the world's best specialists organized in a virtual think tank which generates, studies and evaluates practical ideas about immigration and integration policies. MPI, together with members of the Management Board and the policy partners (the Bertelsmann Stiftung and the European Policy Centre), systematically promote Council findings and decisions.

The Council is transatlantic at its very core because policymakers in Europe and North America face increasingly similar migration-related issues. As a result, policymakers find themselves coordinating more closely in areas which, only a few years ago, were considered to be sovereign prerogatives, especially concerning mobility and security matters. They are more interested in exchanging policy ideas and good practice across the entire migration policy and practice continuum: expanding legal migration channels across skills and types (permanent, temporary, contract, project-tied, etc.) of movements, more effective integration and better relations between newcomers and established communities; exploring the idea of forging an agenda on migration and development. Furthermore, there is a growing awareness that the actions of governments on either side of the Atlantic have implications for each other in areas such as the prevention of terrorist travel, responses to radicalization, the evolution (some say "subversion") of the idea of citizenship and the risk that popular (but poorly reasoned) ideas of migration management will spread across the Atlantic.

The Council aims to help policymakers map the landscape with robust, analytically anchored ideas and thus inform, and even shape, the transatlantic policy agenda on migration.

The History of the Transatlantic Council on Migration

The Transatlantic Council on Migration succeeds the Transatlantic Task Force on Immigration and Integration, which was launched in the spring of 2006 by MPI and the Bertelsmann Stiftung. A full description of the Task Force, its members, publications and events is available at: www.migrationpolicy.org/transatlantic/.

The Task Force's mission was to work closely with, and thus influence, the EU-wide policies advanced by the European Union presidencies of Germany and Portugal in 2007. On behalf of the Task Force, MPI served as key advisor to both presidencies and developed the substantive content for EU ministerial meetings in their entirety.

Working cooperatively with the EU Parliament and the European Commission, the Task Force placed on the EU agenda recommendations related to several critical areas, including: how citizenship policies affect integration and social cohesion; the relationship between states and emerging religious communities; the role of education in integration; and the need to re-conceptualize migration policies to improve both the economic goals of the Member States and the EU-wide development goals.

The Task Force also brought together leaders of Muslim communities, thinkers on Muslim-state relations and senior transatlantic policy officials to discuss vital differences—and find common ground—on the question of radicalization. The Task Force completed its work at the end of 2007.

The Task Force's experience has richly informed the conceptualization of the Council. The lessons learned are reflected both in the framing of the concept and its implementation—and these can be seen not only in the breadth and ambition of the effort, but also in the targeted focus of the mission statement, its broader geographic reach and its commitment to the wide dissemination of the Council's work.

The Operation of the Transatlantic Council on Migration

The Migration Policy Institute, working closely with the Council's Management Board and its policy partners (the Bertelsmann Stiftung and the European Policy Centre) will be responsible for all of the Council's work and activities. Brief dossiers will be prepared that summarize and dissect potential Council issues, and outline the political and policy opportunities presented by each between now and 2010.

The Management Board is composed of relevant MPI staff and representatives of the Council's financial supporters. It meets annually to plan the following year's work, examining and commissioning research in consultation with Council Members and key government policymakers.

The full Council meets twice annually and all meetings are held under the Chatham House Rule, designed to foster openness and the free exchange of information. Smaller preparatory and expert sessions are held prior to each meeting. The European Policy Centre will also hold two meetings per year to ensure that policymakers in Brussels are exposed to the Council's ideas. The Council plans additional satellite meetings and extraordinary meetings as warranted. Extraordinary meetings of interested Council members are convened in the capital of the country that is consulting the Council at any one time. Such meetings focus on issues of particular concern to the host country and/or are in response to an immigration crisis.

In 2008, the full Council meetings were hosted by the Rockefeller Foundation in Bellagio, Italy (April) and the Greentree Foundation in New York (November).

Attendance at each meeting is carefully constructed. Together with permanent Council members, who are the overall effort's motivating force and principal constituents, each Council meeting will be enriched by the presence of senior policymakers and senior policy advisors (who are usually involved in drafting and implementing initiatives in the areas of the Council's work), and one or more top experts on the specific issue(s) on the agenda. In addition, each meeting will typically include a few select political and business leaders. Civil society and community leaders will also be asked to observe and address Council meetings, as appropriate. As a matter of course, the Council will invite two or three senior journalists and writers to each Council session, so that they can gain more insight into migration issues and so that the Council may benefit from their experience. Any reporting that flows from their participation will strictly follow the Chatham House Rule.

The First Meeting of the Transatlantic Council on Migration

The Council was launched in April 2008 at the Rockefeller Foundation Conference Center in Bellagio, Italy. The meeting focused on two themes: (1) Migration and Development and (2) Identity and Citizenship in the 21st Century.

The first two days of the Council meeting in April were dedicated to an expert-led session on migration and development. The Council focused on two contested but promising themes in this area: (a) the effects of diasporas on development and (b) how countries can best negotiate bilateral and other agreements that allow for greater legal mobility and the advancement of development goals.

The second theme, Identity and Citizenship in the 21st Century, was the Council's plenary theme. Several key issues were addressed under this rubric, including: the importance of local voting rights and civic engagement/participation rights for immigrants; trends in dual citizenship and the implications for immigrant integration and broader social cohesion; and the rationale for, and implications of, the tightening of residency and naturalization requirements.

An abbreviated summary of the discussion that took place during the first meeting of the Council is included in this book.

Dissemination

The Council makes use of a variety of dissemination outlets, most obviously in the production of this book.

Each Council meeting concludes with a Council statement prepared by MPI with its policy partners. This statement will be disseminated via the media, in private briefings of senior politicians, in public briefings, in workshops organized by partner institutions and in conversational contacts.

The Council also will make wide use of online dissemination, tapping into the extensive databases of MPI and its partners, as well as into MPI's award-winning and widely-read online journal "Migration Information Source".

Next Steps and Future Meetings

The Transatlantic Council on Migration will embark on the theme of "International Competitiveness and the Future of Migration", whose organizing principle is to investigate the relationship between migration and competitiveness.

We aim to connect the global dots between major demographic trends in countries of the developing world (notably China, India and Africa) and in the countries of Europe and North America. We will begin by examining three crucial components: (a) the movement of people to and from the transatlantic space, (b) how this connects to the investments we must make in key domestic and immigration policies and (c) policies to improve competitiveness.

In the second Council meeting, scheduled for November 2008, we will start to map the demographics and look into the question of skills and talent by exploring work on the main emigration and immigration trends from China and India to Europe and North America. We will also discuss work on selection systems and on conceptualizing the movement of talented people.

Council Statement: Delivering Citizenship

Demetrios G. Papademetriou, Annette Heuser, Hans Martens

The Transatlantic Council on Migration is a unique deliberative body that examines vital policy issues and informs migration policy-making processes across the Atlantic community. The Council takes a non-partisan, evidence-based, pragmatic approach that is ardently independent. It has a dual mission:

1. To help inform, and thus influence, the transatlantic immigration and integration agendas by proactively identifying, analyzing and drawing out the policy insights of critical issues and bringing them to public attention.
2. To serve as an idea factory and resource for governments as they grapple with the challenges and opportunities associated with international migration.

Council members and Council guests combine exceptional political, policy, and public influence with profound interest, experience and expertise in issues relating to migration. Each year, the Council holds two meetings to examine a key aspect of international migration. The meetings are supported by commissioned research and policy analysis, supplemented by expert presentations.

The Council releases a statement twice a year on a migration topic. Each statement is the result of a series of judgments made by the Council, informed both by the commissioned research and the Council's discussions. The purpose of each Transatlantic Council Statement is to present a series of evidence-based options to a senior political and policy audience.

The Council Statement is the sole responsibility of the Migration Policy Institute and its policy partners [the Bertelsmann Stiftung and the European Policy Centre (in cooperation with the King Baudouin Foundation)]. It reflects the discussions of the Council but the final responsibility for content rests with the authors.

This is the Council's first Statement.

Defining Citizenship and Its Purpose

Citizenship—once a narrow, largely placid legal backwater—has become a dynamic policy vehicle for promoting the political incorporation of immigrants and, by extension, their more complete integration. Greater attention to the issue in recent years has led to the proliferation of tests and other requirements associated with citizenship.

Countries in North America and Europe are redesigning, modifying and evaluating citizenship policy and practice. The Council noted that governments conceive of citizenship differently and they should not conflate ends with means. Clarifying definitions, broad goals and desired outcomes is critical when designing and implementing effective citizenship policies that meet the needs of society as a whole.

The Council's view coalesced around the proposition that we cannot all agree on the boundaries of citizenship, but we can confirm its center. The "core" definition of citizenship is equal membership in a self-governing political community, comprising four layers:

1. Formal legal status that links individuals to a state or polity.
2. A set of legal rights and duties. Rights include civil liberties and the right of representation, as well as social rights to education, health care and poverty protection. Duties include an understanding of the constitution, jury service obligations and loyalty to the state (most obviously sought in times of international conflict).
3. A set of responsibilities and practices that support a rules-based democratic self-government.
4. A collective identity that can be shared across distinctions of income, class, race, gender, religion, ethnic origin or lifestyle.

The above definition highlights the need to place citizenship policy and practice into a broader context: citizenship policies are not interchangeable with immigrant integration policies. While citizenship offers fundamental protections that are not available through integration, there are elements of integration policy—such as access to education and employment—that are arguably more important for success in society.

Principles

The Council's overall judgment concerning citizenship policy is that it should emphasize inclusion and contribute to societal cohesion.

Accordingly, a key goal for policymakers in delivering citizenship policies is to make citizenship meaningful and inclusive. To achieve this goal requires adopting policies that reflect the different migration contexts of countries yet are nonetheless decidedly inclusive.

The Council contends that:

- Citizenship is a crucial right and should be regarded as such by governments and citizens alike. However, while it should be clearly accessible to immigrants and thus serve as an incentive for greater integration, citizenship should not be thought of as the principal tool for immigrant integration or, for that matter, as the end point of the integration process.

- Governments must understand the value of citizenship and communicate this awareness to new immigrants and the native population alike. Among other things, citizenship bestows: security (such as protection from a variety of governmental actions, including deportation); unfettered access to labor markets; access to public services (including social rights to education, health care and all the benefits that society offers); and rights for families. Citizenship also facilitates travel, a benefit of high and increasing consequence.

- While governments should try to make the citizenship process meaningful, they also need to recognize that this can have counterproductive effects if the hurdles to acquiring citizenship are set too high. There is a public interest in naturalization processes that are fair and transparent.

- New immigrants should be seen as potential new citizens early on in the migration process or at least be placed on the first rungs of a ladder that leads to integration and full citizenship. While some immigrants might not ultimately complete the citizenship process, assuming that they might do so is the best starting point for constructing policy.

This perspective invites policymakers to consider citizenship in inclusive terms and begin integration efforts early. Legitimate policy and legal barriers to citizenship (for example in the case of temporary workers or university students who do not have a right to permanent residence) must be understood in this context.

Actions

There is no single path to citizenship, even within a single country. Yet there are a number of common issues that can be addressed by all governments, regardless of historical and political contexts. The Council notes that there are several forks in the road where guidance is useful, for example regarding questions of: local voting during the pre-citizenship stage; whether to introduce civics tests or test for language skills; and finally, whether to permit the acquisition of dual citizenship.

The Council acknowledges these are contentious issues and recognizes the high-wire act policymakers must walk on citizenship policy. The Council advises that:

- Citizenship policy should be meaningful and practical, and should encourage all new immigrants to seek naturalization as soon as their status allows. As such, governments should ensure that all barriers relating to costs are kept as low as possible.
- Local voting rights encourage immigrants to participate in local politics and offer them a safety valve; and at the same time offer a

mechanism to signal acceptance of immigrants to society in general. Such rights also encourage political parties to think at the earliest possible time about the changing composition of their electoral base—and to become more inclusive where it matters most, namely at the grassroots level. On the other hand, local voting rights do not radically improve voting turnout among non-citizens and have only minor effects on the later acquisition of citizenship.

- Language tests can be a positive part of the integration and citizenship process. Thus, linking language learning to citizenship can be a useful impetus for migrants to become involved in other parts of society. Learning the host language helps immigrants reduce their economic and social isolation, and is an essential tool for their success in the job market. However, a balance should be struck between offering immigrants adequate and meaningful opportunities for learning the host language and setting requirements that deter them from learning it—thereby undermining the overall policy's goals by increasing the likelihood of social, cultural and economic marginalization. If the ability to speak the host language is made a condition of citizenship, governments must provide sufficient opportunities and resources for learning it.

- Civics tests can add value to the citizenship process and provide immigrants with important practical information. However, they should not be punitive measures, neither by intention nor by the effects they produce. Civics tests should (a) emphasize practical information, (b) be carried out as objectively as possible, (c) be constantly evaluated and adjusted to deliver better outcomes; and (d) use the metric of a high pass rate to gauge success. Over-complication and an over-reliance on cultural norms and customs should be avoided.

- Citizenship ceremonies can contribute to a sense of belonging and pride among newcomers. They offer "common ground" with established citizens, which can bridge divides and encourage interaction among different groups. Citizenship ceremonies should also involve the host community to the highest degree possible. Holding ceremonies in local community settings and events, and ensuring the participation of prominent political leaders, are two ways of doing this.

- Dual citizenship is an increasing reality in our global, mobile world and should not be discouraged. Governments should view dual citizenship also through the lens of the rights and duties of their own expatriates and concentrate on settling contentious matters—such as voting rights and disagreements over jurisdiction—through bilateral and international cooperation.

Policymakers are increasingly looking to citizenship as a dynamic policy vehicle to promote immigrant integration, but questions remain as to whether governments themselves are flexible enough in how they deliver citizenship policies and whether their policies enhance cohesion and advance other societal goals. Yet the importance of finding the right policies and implementing them in a fair and transparent manner is self-evident. The well-being and vibrancy of societies is maximized when all participants, whether native-born or newcomers, feel a sense of belonging. Delivering citizenship in ways that advance these goals is a challenge that must be met if immigrant-receiving countries are to succeed socially and economically.

Part II: Citizenship and Inclusion

Stakeholder Citizenship:
An Idea Whose Time Has Come?

Rainer Bauböck

Democracy is government accountable to its citizens, and states are territorial jurisdictions. International migration creates a tension between these two basic facts about our world because it produces citizens living outside the country whose government is supposed to be accountable to them and inside a country whose government is not accountable to them. The result is a mismatch between citizenship and the territorial scope of legitimate political authority. In response to this challenge, political theorists have occasionally considered how to redraw the boundaries of political community, a problem that has rarely troubled policymakers or voters.

But times have changed. Citizenship policies, which used to be fairly stable and supported by cross-party consensus in many countries, have become thoroughly politicized and volatile. In immigrant-receiving democracies, citizenship policies are now driven by anxieties over security risks and failed integration of newcomers, while a growing number of sending countries are actively reaching out to their expatriates by offering them dual citizenship and absentee-voting rights.

The new emphasis on citizenship as a shared core identity in democratic polities should be welcomed. It adds an important political dimension to past debates about the economic and cultural impacts of migration. However, the interests and ideologies that drive current public concerns are often extremely myopic in three ways: they do not rely on principles that take into account all interests affected; they do not look across borders; and they disregard the counterproductive effects of the policies advocated.

31

This paper addresses such deficits by proposing a stakeholder principle that should guide citizenship policies in Europe and North America. This principle applies to both immigrants and emigrants. Stakeholders in this sense are those who have a stake in the polity's future because of the circumstances of their lives. The paper begins with a definition of democratic citizenship and a discussion of the link between human rights and citizenship. It then considers alternative principles for determining a polity's citizens and argues that stakeholdership is the most attractive concept. After laying these foundations, the paper explores how this principle applies to the acquisition of citizenship at birth and through naturalization. It suggests that a residence-based status of "denizenship" cannot fully substitute for access to citizenship. Finally, it argues that European countries can make a politically acceptable argument for the reform of citizenship laws that could be supported from a stakeholder perspective.

Defining Democratic Citizenship

Citizenship is a concept with multiple dimensions. It is impossible to encompass all of its uses and meanings in a single definition. It is also pointless to try and do so since many interpretations of citizenship are metaphorical or overstretched.

While we cannot define the concept's boundaries, it is possible to define its center. At its core, citizenship is about equal membership in a self-governing political community. Four interpretations of citizenship are directly connected to this core meaning and spell out its implications in the context of modern democracies.

Citizenship is:

1. a formal legal status that links individuals to a state or another established polity (such as the European Union or a federal province);
2. a bundle of legal rights and duties associated with this status, including civil liberties, rights to democratic representation and social rights to education, health care and protection from poverty risks;

3. a set of responsibilities, virtues and practices that support democratic self-government;
4. a collective identity that can be shared across distinctions of class, race, gender, religion, ethnic origin or way of life.

Taken together, these four aspects make up democratic citizenship; taken separately, they also apply to other political formations. For example, in international law, the legal status of citizenship is usually called nationality and refers equally to the subjects of authoritarian regimes and the citizens of democratic ones. Nationality in this sense is a thin form of citizenship that does not entail any normative principles. By contrast, a more comprehensive notion of democratic citizenship requires specific answers to the question: Who has a claim to protection of his or her rights and by which political authority?

However, the link between the four elements is not a straightforward one, even in democratic states. The status of long-term resident foreign nationals who live in democratic countries provides an illustration. Their rights are derived from residence rather than from formal membership, creating a quasi-citizenship ("denizenship"). As a result, historic privileges of citizenship, including the right to vote in local elections in 12 Member States of the European Union, have been extended to long-term resident third-country nationals. More recently, some states have also experimented with offering quasi-citizenship status to emigrants who have lost or renounced their citizenship or to ethnic-kin minorities living in neighboring countries.

A second important distinction must be drawn between the formal/legal and informal aspects of citizenship. As the core definition implies, democratic citizenship is produced by citizens themselves and only indirectly by the state authorities who act on their behalf. It is therefore important to realize that states can regulate some dimensions of citizenship but not others.

Legislators decide on the norms that govern citizenship as a legal status and a bundle of rights and duties. Yet they should not try to legislate the ethical responsibilities, virtues and practices of good citizenship or the collective identities that citizens share as members of the polity. Important as these dimensions are for sustaining democracy over time, political authorities can only promote them indirectly by building institutions that allow individuals to develop the habits and identities of good citizenship. Where state institutions try to do this directly, either by enforcement or exclusion, democracy becomes illiberal and ultimately tyrannical. This is a historic lesson that should have been learned from the French Revolution. It applies to contemporary efforts in several European countries, such as the Netherlands or Great Britain, that test immigrants with regard to their civic virtues and attitudes before granting them citizenship.

This text focuses specifically on citizenship as a legal status. It explores what the core meaning of citizenship as equal membership in a self-governing political community implies for the question of who ought to be included and who can be legitimately excluded from the status of citizenship.

A Human Right to Citizenship

A starting point for this inquiry is the human right to citizenship. Analyzing the plight of refugees and stateless people in the wake of World War II, political theorist Hannah Arendt called citizenship "the right to have rights". In her view, there was a paradox at the heart of the idea of universal human rights: The most fundamental of these rights could only be effectively protected once a state had recognized a human being as his or her citizen.

The paradox could in principle be resolved by including a right to citizenship in the catalogue of human rights. This is what the Universal Declaration of Human Rights of 1948 accomplished. Article 15 states that "everyone has a right to a nationality" and "no one shall be arbitrarily deprived of his nationality nor denied the right to change his nationality". Yet the protection of individuals against statelessness and coercively imposed citizenship does not obligate states to offer their citizenship to individuals whom another state recognizes as citizens.

The Stakeholder Principle of Citizenship

To respond to the mismatch between territorial borders and boundaries of membership, we need to know which individuals have claim to which citizenship. If we define citizenship as equal membership in a self-governing political community, then the most plausible answer to this question is that all those, and only those individuals, who have a stake in the future of a politically organized society have a moral claim to be recognized as its citizens and to be represented in democratic self-government.

The individual rights and well-being of stakeholders are tied to those of other members because they all depend on the protection and public benefits provided by the same political institutions. Stakeholdership in this sense is not a matter of individual choice, but is determined by basic facts of an individual's biography, such as having grown up in a particular society, being a long-term resident there or having close family members in another country where one does not presently reside.

Three Alternatives to the Stakeholder Principle

A stakeholder principle for determining who has a claim to citizenship differs in important ways from alternative answers to the question: Who ought to be included and who can be legitimately excluded from citizenship? A first response says that the decision whom to admit as a citizen is not a moral question. Rather, it is a matter of sovereign self-determination for each state. According to this logic, becoming a citizen is similar to joining a club: just as a club can adopt its own statute for admitting new members, so every state can choose its new citizens.

However, this view is implausible because, in liberal democracies, even social clubs may no longer discriminate in their admission policies on grounds of race, gender or ethnic origin. Since states are responsible for protecting much more fundamental interests and rights of individuals under their jurisdiction, they cannot claim powers to make arbitrary decisions in matters of citizenship—even when these decisions reflect the preferences of a majority of current members.

The implications of the stakeholder view become clearer when we contrast it with two more plausible alternatives: (1) that everybody subjected to the laws should also be represented in the making of the laws and (2) that democracies must offer citizenship to all whose interests are affected by their legislation.

The first of these two principles requires that all current residents (and maybe even temporary visitors) must be included, while those who leave the territory for an extended period have no further claim to retain citizenship status or to participate. This idea includes too many inside the territory and wrongly excludes all those outside the territory. It is also at odds with current laws in all democratic states, which permit emigrants to retain their citizenship and even to pass it on to a next generation born abroad. Moreover, since World War II, the vast majority of democratic states have introduced external voting rights for expatriates, which would seem clearly illegitimate under a strict principle of territorial inclusion.

The second "all affected interests" principle could easily account for emigrants' citizenship. Many expatriates have ongoing ties and are interested in returning to their country of origin at some point, so political decisions taken there affect some of their fundamental interests. However, the principle would also provide native populations of distant countries—whose interests are affected by policies on foreign relations, trade or industrial emissions of another state—with a claim to citizenship in that country.

Even within the domestic territory, democratic legitimacy of decisions is not achieved through representing the interests affected, since this would require constantly modifying the composition of the legislature depending on which citizens would be affected by a particular piece of legislation. Instead, representative democracy means that citizens empower elected legislators to vote on a broad range of issues that affect various groups in different ways.

Why the Stakeholder Principle Makes Sense

The stakeholder principle differs from alternative views of democratic inclusion because it applies to individuals who have a permanent interest in membership and political participation rather than in particular decisions. All long-term residents can be seen to share such an interest because of their permanent subjection to a territorial political authority. But first-generation emigrants and minor children born abroad can also claim a stake in the polity's future if their life prospects depend on that country's laws and political course.

This interpretation of stakeholder citizenship leads to a straightforward conclusion: If resident foreigners enjoy a claim to be admitted as new citizens and emigrants a claim to retain their citizenship of origin, then, as is increasingly the case, both receiving and sending countries ought to tolerate dual citizenship.

However, the problem of mismatch cannot be resolved by simply turning every migrant into a dual citizen. Article 15 of the Universal Declaration of Human Rights supplements the principle of stakeholder inclusion with an element of individual choice. Emigrants must be free to renounce their citizenship provided they acquire another one abroad, and immigrants cannot be forced to become naturalized as long as they have another citizenship.

In liberal democracies exposed to migration, the consequence is that many people are not fully included although they have an individual claim to citizenship. This means that the stakeholder principle must apply beyond the allocation of citizenship as a legal status. In a more general sense, denizens are dual citizens, too, because their overall bundle of rights and duties is jointly produced by the laws of two independent states.

The short answer to the problem of boundary mismatch is therefore that citizenship status and rights ought to be extended to all persons whose personal fate is tied to the long-term prospects of a particular polity. Migration generates overlapping sets of persons to whom this principle applies. If the states connected through migratory chains are liberal democracies, they ought to include immigrants as well as emigrants in their conception of political community while respecting individual choices of primary affiliation.

Furthermore, since more than one state is involved in migrants' citizenship status, governments should coordinate their citizenship policies so as to avoid unjustified exclusion or inclusion. Coordination would also prevent conflicts between their respective territorial jurisdictions over residents and personal jurisdiction over emigrants.

Citizenship and Global Justice

The United Nations classifies less then four percent of the world's population as migrants. Most individuals acquire citizenship at birth and retain it all of their lives. From a global perspective, the most fundamental moral question to ask about citizenship policies is how birthright citizenship determines the opportunities of human beings worldwide.

Political theorist Joseph Carens has suggested that in today's world, citizenship is like feudal status in medieval societies. The citizenship that people are born with pervasively determines their prospects in life; and through immigration control, rich and secure states are able keep out those born as citizens of poor, authoritarian or violence-ridden countries.

This is a morally troubling analogy. Yet its implications are not obvious. Should liberal states open their doors to free immigration? Or do they instead have a responsibility to improve the lives of citizens in the worst-off countries? If one accepts a positive answer to the latter question as being the more plausible, do rich countries have to redistribute their wealth until opportunities have been equalized worldwide? Such a demanding standard for global justice would be hard to reconcile with the fact that citizens and their representatives are committed to improving opportunities in their own countries. The British political theorist David Miller has suggested, therefore, that global justice does not require the equalizing of opportunities through immigration or the redistribution of wealth, but rather through assisting disadvantaged societies to achieve the minimum standards of decency that enable them to secure all their citizens' basic needs.

Moreover, unlike feudal status, citizenship in democratic countries is an institution that supports important moral values of individual liberty, equality and collective self-government within a territorially bounded society. Birthright citizenship specifically secures the continuity of democratic polities across multiple generations. Sustainable democracy requires not merely stable institutions, but also a stable core population whose members have been raised as citizens and who conceive of their future and that of their children as being linked with this particular country.

Territorial democracy, as we know it, could not work in nomadic societies. A society composed of individual nomads of different origins, but without shared citizenship, would be anarchic, socioeconomically unequal and violent. In our world, migrants enter or leave state territories. They can stretch their affiliations across international borders, but they cannot carry their own political authorities with them and establish them wherever they go.

Acquiring Citizenship at Birth

Birthright citizenship can be acquired through descent (*jus sanguinis*) or birth in the territory (*jus soli*). These rules are complementary rather than alternative. Virtually every country in the world applies *jus sanguinis*, which was first introduced into Europe with the French Revolution. In a much smaller number of countries, such as the United States, Canada and Australia, birth in the territory is the dominant principle, and citizenship by descent applies there only to children born to expatriates.

Several European states have modified their *jus sanguinis* regimes by a conditional form of *jus soli*. In some countries, acquisition through birth in the territory depends on the parents' legal status or length of residence (Germany, Ireland, Portugal, the United Kingdom); in others, such as Belgium, France, the Netherlands, Portugal and Spain, a parent must have been born in the country for the child to become a citizen at birth. In several European states (Belgium, Finland, France, Italy, the Netherlands, the UK) citizenship for the second generation is generally not acquired automatically at birth but depends on parental decision after birth or is granted at the age of majority.

In the absence of international migration, the difference between *jus sanguinis* and *jus soli* does not matter. Both secure the intergenerational reproduction of a territorial citizenry. It is migration across state borders that makes a pure regime of *jus sanguinis* exclusionary. The children of settled immigrants who grow up in the receiving country are clearly stakeholders in that society's future. From this perspective, denying them citizenship or even requiring them to undergo a procedure of naturalization is indefensible. They are members of society from birth and ought to be recognized as such.

However, the US model of nearly unconditional *jus soli*, embedded in the 14th Amendment to the Constitution, is not necessarily the best alternative. First, its historic roots go back to post-Civil War Reconstruction, when the government was concerned with making sure former slaves and their children were granted citizenship; the constitutional amendment had nothing to do with immigration. Second, it attributes citizenship to children whose birth in the territory is accidental. That child's parents may raise the child to adulthood in another country, but the child will have a lifelong right to live, work and vote in the United States. Third, American *jus soli* does not include those who arrive with their parents at a very young age. Such children must wait until age 18 before they are eligible to become naturalized and in the meantime their residence status remains insecure.

Today, there is no prospect of introducing the American model to any European country. Ireland, the only European state that had adopted it (also for reasons unrelated to immigration) abandoned it in 2004, after voters overwhelmingly passed a referendum that eliminated an Irish-born child's automatic right to citizenship when the parents are not Irish nationals. Today, such children will be Irish citizens by birth only if one parent has been a legal resident for three out of the last four years.

Combining automatic acquisition at birth for children of settled immigrant parents with the Swedish model—which offers unconditional citizenship to minor children after five years of residence—best captures the idea of stakeholder entitlements. Recent reforms in Germany and Portugal show that such ideas can also win sufficient political support.

In Western Europe, public attention is currently focused on selecting the right kind of immigrants who are "worthy" of naturalization. Only extreme anti-immigrant forces argue openly, however, that children born in the country should be excluded because of their descent. Political efforts to introduce or extend an appropriate form of *jus soli* could therefore have a reasonable chance of success even under current conditions.

The Proliferation of Multiple Citizenship

Birthright citizenship, rather than lenient conditions for naturalization, is also the main cause for the proliferation of multiple citizenship. Children are born as dual citizens when their parents are of different nationalities or when a foreign citizenship acquired by descent adds to a domestic one obtained through *jus soli*. In this way, inclusive rules for birthright citizenship produce overlapping memberships.

Yet several European states still cling to the idea that dual citizenship is an irregularity. The German case illustrates the absurd effects of attempts to adopt liberal rules for citizenship while constraining dual nationality. Currently, Germany has three categories of dual citizens: descendants of parents of different nationalities, those born in Germany to long-term resident foreign parents and those who were granted permission to retain a previous nationality when they became naturalized because renouncing it would have been impossible or unreasonably hard. The first and third categories can keep their two citizenships indefinitely, while those born in Germany to long-term resident foreign parents have to choose a single citizenship status when they are between age 18 and 23. Because of a retroactive application of the *jus soli* reform of 2000, there will soon be cases of young adults who have spent all their lives in Germany but will be stripped of their German citizenship unless they return their second passport.

While a regime of pure *jus sanguinis* is exclusionary in immigrant-receiving societies, it becomes over-inclusive in source countries of emigration. Seven of the 15 old EU Member States and all 12 countries that have joined since 2004 permit their emigrants to transfer their nationality from generation to generation without any residence requirement in the country of origin. A number of states also offer extraterritorial naturalization to persons whom they consider ethnic kin because their ancestors emigrated from that country or because their homeland was once part of the state territory.

Individuals claiming citizenship in these ways are often mainly interested in acquiring a European Union passport that gives them visa-free access to the United States and all EU Member States rather than in "returning" to a country of distant origin. A stakeholder criterion suggests, therefore, that *jus sanguinis* should not apply automatically beyond the first generation born abroad, and that naturalization should generally require a prior period of residence in the country.

Testing for Citizenship: Europe's Problematic Approach to Naturalization

Although the acquisition of citizenship at birth raises important questions, naturalization is at the center of current political debates. The background for these debates is a widespread perception, which is stronger in Europe than in the United States, that the integration of newcomers is not working as it should. There are good reasons to be concerned about long-term unemployment, low educational achievements and segregated housing for groups of migrant origin. In Europe, immigrant integration is rightly seen as a public policy concern rather than as a problem that civil society can take care of without state support and interference. But a strange discrepancy has emerged between a laissez-faire regime of free movement for EU citizens—which has surged since the 2004 and 2007 enlargements despite labor-market restrictions in most Member States—and the heavy-handed control approach toward third-country nationals. EU citizens migrating in large numbers from Poland and Romania to Britain, Ireland, Italy and Spain face similar social, economic, linguistic and cultural challenges of integration as third-country nationals from outside the EU. For this latter category of migrants, a growing number of European countries have introduced integration courses and tests as a condition for access to citizenship, permanent residence, and even for family reunification in the host society. None of these conditions apply to EU citizens.

What purpose is served by such tests? Are they meant to encourage immigrants to acquire linguistic skills and general knowledge about the history and public institutions of their society of residence? Or is their goal to select those worthy of becoming citizens and keep out the rest? Current European governments differ in how they regard the contribution of naturalization to immigrant integration. Some countries, such as Sweden, see it as a step or tool to achieve this larger goal, whereas others, such as Austria or the Netherlands, regard naturalization as the endpoint and ultimate reward for individual success in this process. These two views are hard to reconcile. Raising the hurdles for access to denizenship and citizenship will exacerbate the problems of socioeconomic or cultural integration if the groups who are excluded remain in the country in an insecure legal status. Forced mass return to countries of origin is not only morally indefensible but, for the time being, also politically unfeasible. Therefore, exclusion from citizenship contributes to the very problems that harsher integration tests are meant to address.

The opposite policy of actively promoting naturalization does not rule out using tests as incentives for acquiring additional skills rather than as deterrents from applying. What is needed in this regard is not merely a fine-tuning of conditions for naturalization, but a general change in public philosophies of citizenship.

So far, all European countries regard naturalization as a legal procedure by which an individual attempts to improve her or his legal status, while state authorities—in selecting who gets membership in the polity—have the task of ensuring that the applicant meets criteria determined by public interests. The mismatch between the citizenry and the permanent residents subjected to the laws suggests, however, that democracies also have a public interest in promoting naturalization to avoid a growing deficit of democratic legitimacy.

This consideration of democratic legitimacy makes integration tests problematic, especially when their deterrent effects result in declining numbers of naturalizations, as has been the case following the recent reforms in Austria and the Netherlands. The same critique applies also to a host of other conditions for naturalization, including very common ones, such as proof of independent income and absence of any criminal record. In the 19th century, most European democracies excluded from voting those adults who did not have enough income or property to pay taxes. Immigration countries may want to make sure that persons initially admitted for employment purposes do not end up on public welfare. But if such individuals later become welfare recipients and meet the permanent-residence conditions for naturalization, how can one justify denying them political representation?

Similarly, most democracies deny voting rights to prison inmates. However, once they have served their sentence, former criminals must be readmitted to full citizenship. In many European states, immigrants who commit even minor offenses are never permitted to become naturalized. The rationale behind this exclusion is that citizenship status protects immigrants from deportation. But if the crime is not severe enough to justify deportation before the individuals become naturalized, how can it be severe enough to exclude the person from becoming a citizen? And how does retaining such people in a non-citizen-resident status improve domestic security?

The principle of stakeholder inclusion is therefore incompatible with viewing citizenship as a special reward for individual achievements and with selecting those candidates whose contributions will yield the greatest public benefits. European countries cast aside these criteria when they gradually expanded citizenship to previously excluded domestic groups, such as women, former slaves and paupers.

There is no reason why these criteria should still be regarded as legitimate when applied to immigrants.

Why Denizenship Cannot Replace Citizenship

One objection to the line of reasoning given in the previous section is that immigrants can be excluded from citizenship as long as they are offered the alternative status of denizenship, which includes most of the rights of citizens. This argument fails for two reasons.

First, there are only four countries (Chile, Malawi, New Zealand and Uruguay) that offer all long-term residents voting rights in national elections, and even in these cases various restrictions apply. So the democratic representation deficit persists in the absence of high naturalization rates. It is also not plausible to claim that granting denizens voting rights in national elections is a matter of democratic justice. If they are entitled and encouraged to become naturalized, then rejecting this offer amounts to much the same thing as not exercising their right to vote.

Second, denizenship depends on living in the territory and is lost with taking up residence elsewhere. An extraterritorial denizenship would be a contradiction in terms. Former denizens may be able to retain for a while the right to return to their country of settlement, but they cannot pass on their status to the next generation born abroad. Denizens are citizens of external countries who enjoy domestic rights derived from residence. They are not stakeholders in an indefinite future of the domestic polity and lifelong members of its intergenerational people.

Denizenship is therefore always only a supplement and never a full substitute for citizenship. This is true for individual migrants, who would be stateless without an external citizenship, and for the political community as a whole, which could not generate joint commitments towards a long-term future if it consisted only of denizens.

Prospects for Stakeholder Citizenship

Stakeholder citizenship is not a utopian idea. It was already spelled out in the 1955 Nottebohm judgment of the International Court of Justice in which the court stated that "nationality is a legal bond having as its basis a social fact of attachment, a genuine connection of existence, interests and sentiments." The same principle is in many ways reflected in current policies of both immigrant-receiving and emigrant-sending states as well as in evolving norms of international law. We find evidence in the growing number of countries tolerating dual citizenship at birth and through naturalization; in the rapid proliferation of voting rights for expatriates and the more modest spread of the local franchise for third-country residents; and in the growing number of EU Member States that have made birth in the territory a criterion for citizenship entitlement.

Yet even in democratic states this principle is still far from being universally respected. Resistance comes, on the one hand, from old notions of state sovereignty and self-determination and, on the other hand, from new fears about security threats and integration failure in immigrant-receiving countries.

Political theorists may argue that restricting access to citizenship for immigrants and their children creates a growing legitimacy deficit for democratic governments. However, this argument is unlikely to impress policymakers who are not accountable to foreign nationals excluded from the franchise through tough citizenship laws. The case for stakeholder access to citizenship must therefore be strengthened by other reasons that will resonate more strongly in the public arena. In the United States and Canada, it is not difficult to find such reasons in their histories as nations built by immigrants. The appeal to national history is less likely to win broad popular support in European countries whose national identities are still perceived as ancient and territorially rooted.

In Europe, the case for liberal citizenship regimes must be made with a view toward the future rather than the past. Europe is not only an ageing continent that needs new immigration for demographic and economic reasons. It has also formed a unique supranational union of states with a common citizenship whose core is a right to free movement across state borders. EU citizenship is derived from Member State nationality. Therefore, each country in the European Union produces EU citizens with a right to admission into all other states. This should be sufficient reason for the different states to coordinate their citizenship policies and adopt common standards.

Of course, such pressure towards harmonization may result in either more liberal or more restrictive legislation. But moving current debates on citizenship reforms to a European level could at least weaken the idea that citizenship is primarily a matter of national self-determination rather than of international cooperation.

On both sides of the Atlantic, there are good conditions for publicly debating the principles that should guide citizenship policies. The idea outlined in this paper can therefore also be defended in the political arena: citizenship should be offered to all those (and only those) who have a stake in the future of the political community.

Further Reading

Rainer Bauböck, Bernhard Perchinig and Wiebke Sievers (eds.). *Citizenship Policies in the New Europe*. Amsterdam University Press, 2007.

Rainer Bauböck, Eva Ersboll, Kees Groenendijk and Harald Waldrauch (eds.). *Acquisition and Loss of Nationality. Policies and Trends in 15 European states*. Vol. 1: Comparative Analyses, Vol. 2: Country Analyses. Amsterdam University Press, 2006.

Rainer Bauböck. "Political Boundaries in a Multilevel Democracy". In *Identities, Affiliations and Allegiances*, edited by Seyla Benhabib and Ian Shapiro. Cambridge University Press, 2007: 85-109.

Rainer Bauböck. Stakeholder Citizenship and Transnational Political Participation: A Normative Evaluation of External Voting. *Fordham Law Review* (75) 5: 2393–2447. 2007.

Linda Bosniak. *The Citizen and the Alien. Dilemmas of Contemporary Membership*. Princeton, NJ: University Press, 2006.

Marc M. Howard. Comparative Citizenship: An Agenda for Cross-National Research. *Perspectives on Politics* (4) 3: 443-455. 2006.

Christian Joppke. Transformation of Citizenship: Status, Rights, Identity. *Citizenship Studies* (11) 1: 37–48. 2007.

Miller, David. *National Responsibility and Global Justice*. Oxford University Press, 2007.

Shachar, Ayelet. *The Birthright Lottery. Citizenship and Global Inequality*. Cambridge, MA: Harvard University Press, 2008 (forthcoming).

Local Voting Rights for Non-Nationals in Europe: What We Know and What We Need to Learn

Kees Groenendijk

Since the 1970s, the issue of granting voting rights in municipal elections to resident non-nationals, both EU nationals and third-country nationals, has been on the European political agenda. Four different but related reasons have prompted the political debate.

First, many immigrants from outside the European Union have lived there for a long period but without acquiring the nationality of the host country (so-called third-country nationals). Second, the governments of EU Member States believe that granting the right to vote to European nationals living in another Member State contributes to more positive attitudes towards the European Union. These reasons have prompted debates on voting rights in all EU Member States at one time or another. Third, the governments of EU Member States wish to involve non-citizen ethnic minorities, either third-country nationals or stateless persons, in local-level decisionmaking. This argument has been relevant to recent debates in Slovenia and Estonia. Finally, the governments of some EU Member States, such as the United Kingdom and Portugal, want to provide a privileged status to immigrants from their former colonies.

This policy brief answers four questions crucial to the local voting rights debate:

1. Which European countries have extended local voting rights to resident third-country nationals and under which conditions?
2. What are the key issues in the political debate?
3. What international instruments will influence future developments?

4. What do we know about the effects of granting voting rights to non-nationals?

In addition, we will address voting rights in terms of immigrant integration policy: Are they an alternative to naturalization or do they complement naturalization? The policy brief concludes with a set of policy recommendations.

The reader should be aware of the limitations of this paper. First, the right to vote in municipal elections is only one (important) part of the larger category of political rights.

Second, the study is restricted to Europe, specifically the 27 EU Member States, Norway and Switzerland. Third, the rights of resident third-country nationals are the primary focus—not EU nationals who live in another EU Member State—because third-country nationals outnumber such EU nationals by almost three to one: 18.5 million of the total non-national population of 27 million are third-country nationals (European Commission 2007: 3). According to EU law, EU nationals who live in another EU Member State have the right to vote in local elections, as well as in those for the European Parliament.

Local Voting Rights across Europe

Of the 29 European states covered in this paper, 17 allow some categories of resident non-nationals to participate in local elections (Waldrauch 2005; Geyer 2007; Oriol 2007). These states are Belgium, Denmark, Estonia, Finland, Hungary, Ireland, Lithuania, Luxembourg, the Netherlands, Norway, Portugal, Slovakia, Slovenia, Spain, Sweden, six cantons in Switzerland and the United Kingdom. Eight of these 17 states (Denmark, Hungary, Norway, Portugal, Slovakia, Sweden, six cantons in Switzerland and the United Kingdom) allow non-nationals (EU nationals and third-country nationals) to vote in elections for regional or national representative bodies. Five of these 17 states (Belgium, Estonia, Hungary, Luxembourg and Slovenia) do not allow third-country nationals to stand as candidates in municipal elections.

The 12 states (of the total 29) that do not allow any voting in local elections are Austria, Bulgaria, Cyprus, Czech Republic, France, Germany, Greece, Italy, Latvia, Malta, Poland and Romania. In the Czech Republic, Italy and Malta, respective constitutional laws permit nonnationals to vote, but the required national legislation or international agreements have not been adopted. Thus, third-country nationals have never participated in local elections in these three countries.

Conditions

States that have granted voting rights to third-country nationals use four kinds of conditions to restrict that right:
- duration of residence,
- registration or application,
- a specific residence status or
- reciprocity (meaning that nationals of country A can vote in country B only if nationals of country B can vote in country A, mostly on the basis of a bilateral agreement between the two countries).

Some states apply two conditions. For example, Belgium requires five years of residence and registration, and Portugal requires reciprocity and registration.

Duration of Residence

The duration of residence required varies between three years in Denmark, Estonia, Norway, Portugal and Sweden and five years in Belgium, Luxembourg and the Netherlands. Finland requires four years for third-country nationals and two years for Nordic citizens (Sweden, Norway and Iceland). In the six relevant Swiss cantons, the residence requirement varies: five years in Appenzell, Fribourg and Neuchâtel; eights years in Geneva; and ten years in Jura and Vaud. Ireland and the United Kingdom do not have a residence requirement.

In the 1990s, the Netherlands tightened its residence conditions, requiring five years of uninterrupted lawful residence. The new requirement caused considerable problems in certain municipalities because the information from the immigration service proved to be incomplete or outdated. Hence, individual immigrants, civil society groups and MPs complained that the government was unlawfully excluding non-national voters from the elections.

Registration or Application

Several states require non-national voters to register with the local authorities. In Ireland and the United Kingdom, a simple registration (comparable to the registration nationals are required to perform) is sufficient. The registration process itself can become a major obstacle for non-nationals who want to exercise their voting rights. Belgium requires non-citizens to file an application for registration and to sign a declaration pledging respect to the Belgian Constitution and legislation. In 2006, the percentage of potential non-national voters that were actually registered varied between 28 percent in the Walloon region, 16 percent in the Flemish region and 14 percent in the Brussels region (Zibouh 2007: 145)

Type of Residence Status

Five states (Estonia, Hungary, Lithuania, Slovakia and Slovenia) do not apply a simple residence requirement; rather they grant voting rights only to third-country nationals who have a permanent residence permit or long-term residence status. This condition may severely limit the number of third-country nationals who can vote since the national governments in these countries grant the required status infrequently or only to specific categories of immigrants (e.g., co-ethnics).

Reciprocity

The Czech Republic, Malta, Portugal and Spain apply the reciprocity condition. In practice, this condition results in far-reaching restriction or de facto non-existence of voting rights. The Czech Republic and Malta have no agreements with third countries. Spain has one relevant agreement, with Norway. Thus, nationals of Norway have been the only non-EU nationals who effectively have the right to vote in Spain. In 2006, the Spanish government announced that it intended to conclude voting-rights agreements with five countries in South America, but no such agreements are yet in force. Portugal has concluded agreements with many countries outside the European Union, adding ten countries alone in recent years.

Key Issues in the Political Debate

When a government grants voting rights to non-nationals, it makes a visible commitment to the public inclusion and equal treatment of immigrants. Within the different states, however, opinions vary on how much immigrant inclusion is desirable and which values are essential for the state's identity (see below).

The main arguments used in favor of extending voting rights to resident non-nationals include the following:

- "No taxation without representation." All members of the community who regularly pay taxes need to be represented in government bodies that decide how public funds are spent and how rules binding on all residents are made.
- Equal treatment over time. The longer non-nationals are resident in a community, the more difficult it is to justify excluding them from the public decision-making process.
- More political participation of the whole society. Granting voting rights stimulates the political participation of immigrants and thus their integration in the host society.

- Immigrants are permanent members of society. Providing voting rights tells the majority of the population that long-term resident immigrants are staying.
- Pathway to citizenship. The right to vote in local elections encourages non-nationals to become naturalized so that they can also vote in national elections and gain access to public service jobs.

The main arguments that opponents give for not allowing non-nationals to vote include the following:
- Voting rights should be an earned privilege. Voting rights are by definition linked to nationality; only full citizens should participate in political decision making.
- Prevent foreign influence. Governments of the origin countries may try to influence the political process through their nationals.
- Prevent ethnic parties. If certain groups of immigrants establish their own political parties, others could form single-issue parties, possibly weakening existing parties.
- Immigrants should not be allowed to disturb power relations. Allowing non-nationals to vote upsets the current balance of power, with some parties benefiting more from the immigrant vote than others.
- The domino effect. Once local voting rights are granted, the argument for withholding voting rights in national elections becomes weaker (although it could be argued that national voting rights could create conflicting loyalties; the same argument is used against dual nationality).
- Encourage naturalization instead. Granting voting rights diminishes immigrants' interest in becoming naturalized.

Some of these arguments have a long history, and have been used to keep workers, women and young citizens from voting.

Voting Rights for Non-Nationals and Images of the State

How someone defines a community or a state will often influence how that person views voting rights for non-nationals. Proponents tend to have a liberal view and an open image of the state. Opponents tend to have a communitarian perspective on the state: only the present members ("citizens") should decide who belongs to a given community. This perspective corresponds to a more closed or defensive image of the nation-state.

The dominant view may change over time. In the politically insecure decade before and after World War II, governments considered the political activity of non-nationals to be dangerous and, in some cases, unlawful. The 1950 European Convention on Human Rights contains a clause providing that nothing in the articles on the freedom of expression, the freedom of association and the non-discrimination clause "shall be regarded as preventing the High Contracting Parties from imposing restrictions on the political activity of aliens" (Article 16). Since then, different states have taken a more open view of statehood. The extension of voting rights described above, the international instruments discussed below, and the development of EU citizenship in 1992 all indicate that the "political activity of aliens" has gradually become acceptable over the past five decades.

Political Debate and Constitutional Obstacles

In several European states, the political debate on local voting rights often resulted in those rights not being granted (Geyer 2007). Constitutional provisions granting voting rights to "the people" or to nationals of the country only proved to be serious obstacles in most cases.

In Germany, the debate continued during most of the 1980s (Sieveking et al. 1989), effectively ending in 1990 when the German Constitutional Court declared the local voting-rights legislation of certain German federal states (Länder) to be unconstitutional. The court argued that the constitutional clause granting voting rights to the German people had to be interpreted as covering only persons with German nationality (Judgment of 13 October 1990. BVerfGE 83: 37). The Constitutional Court of Austria handed down a similar judgment in 2004 (Verfassungsgerichtshof 30 June 2004. C 218/03). In the 1980s, then French President François Mitterand repeatedly promised during election campaigns to introduce local voting rights, but he never put forward any proposal for the required constitutional amendment. In 1992, the Constitutional Council held that it would be contrary to the French Constitution to extend voting rights to non-nationals.

In Italy, a provision granting local voting rights to permanent resident non-nationals was included in the 1998 Immigration Act, but the required amendment to the Italian Constitution was never adopted (Pastore 2001; Grosso 2007). Proposals for local voting rights in Switzerland have been supported by a majority of the electorate in some cantons, but clear majorities rejected such proposals in more than ten cantons between 1993 and 2007 (Giugni 2007).

In Belgium, the debate over voting rights for immigrants started in the early 1970s (Jacobs 1998, 1999). However, Belgium amended its constitution to allow resident EU and third-country nationals to vote only after a ruling in 1998 of a court of justice of the European Community. The court found that Belgium had violated a 1994 Council Directive because it had not yet introduced municipal voting rights for resident EU nationals (Judgment of 8 July 1998, Case C-323/97). Third-country nationals participated in Belgian local elections for the first time in 2006 (Teney and Jacobs 2007; Zibouh 2007).

Alternatives to Extending the Franchise

In several European states (e.g., Germany, Belgium and the Netherlands), the debate on local voting rights has been linked to the debate on naturalization. The German Constitutional Court, in a ruling in 1990, explicitly hinted that the government should make it easier for immigrants to become naturalized instead of giving them the right to vote in local elections. One could view the German Nationality Act, which came into effect in 2000, as a belated realization of the court's suggestion: it introduced *jus soli* acquisition of Germany nationality by the children of settled immigrants and allowed dual nationality for some immigrants (e.g., nationals of other EU Member States).

Belgium and the Netherlands made similar trade-offs between nationality law and voting rights. After the Belgian government liberalized naturalization rules in 2001, the debate on local voting rights abated (Jacobs 2007). In the Netherlands, the Social Democrats (PvDA) and the Christian Democrats (CDA), coalition partners in Parliament, reached a political compromise in the early 1990s. They decided to liberalize naturalization rules, which meant accepting dual citizenship, instead of granting non-nationals the right to vote in provincial and national elections, a policy favored the Social Democrats but strongly opposed by the Christian Democrats.

Examining the Arguments

Ideology-based arguments for and against local voting rights can only be tested in debates. However, one can examine evidence for and against the desired or feared effects of granting such rights.

One observation requires no further research: none of the 17 states that granted local voting rights to non-national residents have abolished this right because of its negative effects, presumed or real. The Swiss canton Neuchâtel introduced voting rights for non-nationals in 1849. Some years later, that right was revoked and then reintroduced in 1875. It still exists today. Since 1988, the anti-immigrant Danish Peoples Party has pleaded repeatedly for restricting the existing voting rights which were granted to non-national residents in Denmark in 1981. But the party has never received support from any other political party (Ostergaard-Nielsen 2007).

Once governments grant local voting rights, these rights never appear as a source of serious conflict. Apparently, most politicians in the countries concerned find that the advantages outweigh any disadvantages. After all, extending voting rights is a low-cost measure. Sharing

political power with an additional group may be symbolically pain-
ful, but in reality power-sharing only marginally reduces the political
power of old voters.

The Influence of International Instruments on
Future Developments

We have focused on the national legislation of 27 European states.
Now we turn to three sets of European rules regarding the right to
vote or other political rights of non-nationals:
1. Local voting rights for EU nationals
2. 2007 Lisbon Reform Treaty
3. 1992 Council of Europe Convention on the Participation of Foreigners in Public Life at the Local Level

It is useful to first look at the Nordic Union, which offers an early
regional consensus on this issue. Denmark, Norway and Sweden
formed the Nordic Passport Union in the 1950s and allowed Nordic
nationals to freely work and live in any Nordic country. Finland and
Iceland joined in 1965. In 1972, Finland raised the issue of voting
rights for Nordic nationals living in another Nordic state. Three years
later, official bodies in Denmark and Sweden advised their governments to introduce voting rights in municipal elections for non-national residents; the Nordic Union published an informative docu-
ment on this issue. In 1977, the Nordic Council reached an informal
consensus and adopted a recommendation stating that Nordic citizens residing in other Nordic states should be able to vote. They did
not sign a formal treaty.[1]

The consensus proved effective. In 1977, Sweden granted local voting rights to all non-nationals with three years of residence. Denmark
and Finland followed suit the same year, with Denmark extending lo-

1 Based on information kindly provided by Jens Vested Hansen, Eva Ersbøll and
   Eeva-Riikka Nykänen.

cal voting rights to all non-national residents in 1981 and Finland doing the same in 1991. Norway granted local voting rights to Nordic nationals in 1978 and to all non-nationals in 1985.

In the long run, granting voting rights only to Nordic citizens led to voting rights for all non-nationals. The Nordic experience has also shown that harmonizing voting rights does not require states to adopt binding laws; informal consensus can work. This lesson could inform the current debates within EU bodies.

Rules on Local Voting Rights of EU Nationals

In the mid-1970s, several European institutions began considering granting local voting rights to nationals from one Member State who are residing in another Member State. Driving these discussions were the idea of a European citizenship and Italy's desire to reinforce the position of its nationals working and living in other Member States.[2] In 1992, Member States agreed in the Maastricht Treaty to add the current Article 19(1) to the Treaty on the European Union. This article grants EU citizens resident in another Member State the right to vote and stand for election under the same conditions as the nationals of the country of residence.

In 1994, the Council of the European Union adopted a directive providing that Member States apply to Member State nationals the same residence requirements for voting and standing for elections as for nationals of their own country.[3] The Member States were expected to implement the provisions of the directive before 1996. The Council granted an exception to Member States in which, in 1996, the proportion of voting-age, non-national EU citizens exceeded 20 percent.

2 See the report of the European Parliament of 25 October 1977, PE 45.833 def, written mainly by MEP Scelba and the European Commission Bulletin supplement 7/75 "To a European citizenship".
3 Council Directive of 19 December 1994 laying down detailed arrangements for the exercise of the right to vote and to stand as a candidate in municipal elections by citizens of the Union residing in a Member State of which they are not nationals, EC Official Journal 1994 L 368, p. 38–47.

Only Luxembourg uses this exception; it requires five years of both for the right to vote and to stand for election. The European Commission considered the use to be justified because the proportion of nationals living in Luxembourg who are from other Member States and of voting age is more than 35 percent (European Commission 2005).

The Lisbon Reform Treaty of 2007

The Constitutional Treaty of 2004, which voters in France and the Netherlands refused to ratify and the European Union has since abandoned, contained two provisions relevant to local voting rights. Article I-10(2)(b) would have copied the right to vote in municipal elections from the current Article 19(1) EC Treaty. Secondly, it contained a new article, Article III-267(4), that would have provided funding for national-level immigrant integration measures.[4]

Both provisions were included in the Reform Treaty that Member States signed in Lisbon in December 2007; the Reform Treaty, also known as the Treaty of Lisbon, essentially replaced efforts to pass a European constitution. Article 17(2) provides that citizens of the Union shall enjoy "(b) the right to vote and to stand as candidates in elections to the European Parliament and in municipal elections in their Member State of residence, under the same conditions as nationals of that State." Moreover, Article 63a(4) of the new treaty provides that the European Parliament and the Council may establish "measures to provide incentives and support for the action of Member States with a view to promoting the integration of third-country nationals residing legally in their territories, excluding any harmonization of the laws and regulations of the Member States."

The European Union has the power to make rules on voting rights for EU nationals and on migration, residence and asylum of third-country nationals in Member States. However, it has no legal authority to make binding rules on the voting rights of third-country nationals

4   EC Official Journal 2004 C 310, p. 13 and 116.

residing in the Member States, as noted in the last phrase of Article 63a(4).

In 2003, the Council of Ministers adopted a directive on the status of long-term, third-country-national residents.[5] This directive codifies denizen status—a status in which long-term resident non-nationals have some but not all of the rights granted to citizens—in EC law. It grants a secure residence right, equal treatment and limited mobility within the European Union to third-country nationals after five years of lawful residence in a Member State. The directive enumerates a long catalogue of matters in which long-term residents shall enjoy equal treatment with nationals, but it does not deal with voting rights. This illustrates that the EC Treaty does not provide a legal basis for obliging Member States to grant voting rights or other political rights to resident third-country nationals. The wording of the directive also shows that certain Member States (e.g., Germany and Austria) are unwilling to grant the European Union authority in this field.

The local voting rights in Article 19(1) of the EC Treaty are explicitly restricted to EU nationals only. However, this does not prevent EU institutions from stimulating legislation that will introduce or extend such rights to third-country nationals. The new provision for funding integration measures could even be used to that end. The European Union can encourage, but not legally oblige, Member States to amend their national laws regarding voting rights for third-country nationals.

The Lisbon Treaty incorporates the EU Charter of Fundamental Rights, which the heads of all EU institutions signed in 2000, into EU law. Articles 11 and 12 of the Charter, like the European Court of Human Rights (ECHR), grant political rights (such as freedom of expression and information, freedom of association and freedom of assembly) to "everyone"—hence to all residents of the Member States, irrespective of their nationality. This language may provide a basis for EU bodies to informally discuss the way certain political rights are

5   Council Directive of 25 November 2003 concerning the status of third-country nationals who are long-term residents, EC Official Journal 2004 L 16, p. 44–53.

structured in the national laws of the Member States. Such discussions could result in recommendations, not in binding EU rules.

The Council of Europe Convention on the Participation of Foreigners in Public Life at the Local Level

On 5 February 1992, the Committee of Ministers of the Council of Europe adopted the "Convention on the Participation of Foreigners in Public Life at the Local Level". All Member States of the Council of Europe, hence also non-EU Member States, may ratify this Convention (Council of Europe Treaty Series No. 144). The Convention deals with several political rights of resident non-nationals, such as the freedoms of expression, assembly and association, and the right to vote. States which have ratified this convention undertake to encourage and facilitate the establishment of consultative bodies representing foreign residents at the local level. The Convention is an implicit amendment of ECHR Article 16, which allows Member States to restrict the political rights of non-nationals. One crucial aspect is that parties to the Convention agree to Article 6, which grants all lawfully resident non-nationals the following: "The right to vote and to stand for elections in local authority elections, provided that he fulfils the same legal requirements as apply to nationals and furthermore has been a lawful and habitual resident in the State concerned for the five years preceding the elections."

States may extend only the right to vote and not the right to stand for elections. Article 7 allows states to opt for a shorter residence requirement.

The Convention came into force in 1995. Eight European states have ratified it, including all five Nordic states, the Netherlands, Italy and Albania. Italy and Albania, however, excluded the provisions on voting rights from their ratifications. Four states (Cyprus, the Czech Republic, Slovenia and the United Kingdom have signed but not ratified the Convention.

The Effects of Granting Voting Rights to Non-Nationals

Crossing the Symbolic Line

In the Nordic countries and the three Benelux countries, the introduction of voting rights for a privileged category of non-nationals (Nordic citizens or EU citizens) resulted in extending these rights to other resident non-nationals, irrespective of their nationality, either at the same time (Sweden and the Netherlands) or some years later (the other five states). Once a state broke the symbolic link between voting rights and nationality, the extension proved politically less problematic.

However, other EU Member States (e.g., Germany, France, Spain and Italy) amended their constitutions to give voting rights only to EU nationals rather than to all resident non-nationals because they had agreed to this provision and nothing more in the 1992 Treaty of Maastricht. In contrast, Ireland and the United Kingdom have long allowed local (and national) voting rights for certain non-nationals, and these practices have provoked little theoretical debate or political opposition.

Actual Use of Voting Rights

Empirical data on the number of non-national or immigrant voters who exercise their voting rights are available for five countries (Denmark, Finland, the Netherlands, Sweden and Switzerland). Data on the number of registered non-national voters are available for three other countries (Belgium, Ireland and Luxembourg). From these data it appears that, generally, non-national voters have lower participation rates in local elections than citizens.

Participation rates vary over time, between cities and between immigrant groups. At times, certain immigrants groups have turned out in proportionally higher numbers than the general population. For instance, Turkish immigrants in Denmark, the Netherlands and Switzerland have had generally higher participation rates than other immigrant groups. It appears that local political circumstances influence the participation rates and voting patterns of non-national voters. The table below illustrates both the differences between migrants groups and the effect of local circumstances.

In the table below, naturalized migrants are included in very small numbers in 1994, but in ever larger percentages in the later years. In 2006, probably the large majority of the voters of Turkish and Moroccan origin were Dutch nationals. These data are the only available long-term data on the voting behaviour of immigrant groups that did not have the nationality of the host country at the time of immigration and, hence, at first could not participate in elections because of their nationality.

Table 1: Turnout of migrant voters in three Dutch cities, 1994 to 2002 (percentage of all eligible)

	Amsterdam				Rotterdam				Arnhem		
Origin country	1994	1998	2002	2006	1994	1998	2002	2006	1994	1998	2006
Turkey	67	39	30	51	28	42	54	56	56	50	54
Morocco	49	23	22	37	23	33	40	58	51	18	52
All voters	57	46	48	51	57	48	55	58	57	52	50

Source: Michon, Tillie and van Heelsum 2007.

Generally, the number of non-national or immigrant municipal councilors elected increases over time according to data from countries that compile this information. In Denmark, the number of councilors with third-country backgrounds increased from 3 in 1981 to 51 in 2001. In Luxembourg, 189 (i.e. 6 percent) of the candidates in the 2005 elections were non-nationals; 14 were elected (Dubajic 2007). More than 300 non-Dutch councilors (4 percent of the total) were elected in the Netherlands' municipal elections in 2006, including 157 of Turkish origin and 66 of Moroccan origin. In Sweden, the foreign born (either naturalized or non-nationals) held 7 percent of the municipal council seats in 2002, twice as many as ten years earlier (Soininen 2007).

Three factors can explain these increases: larger numbers of immigrant voters, the willingness of political parties to place more candidates of immigrant origin on their lists, and a clear preference among immigrant voters for candidates of their own ethnic group.

Voting Rights and Integration

Whether granting voting rights helps immigrants become integrated largely depends on how integration is defined. If integration means the level of participation of immigrants in the central institutions of the host society (e.g., the labor market; schools; religious, military or political institutions), then extending voting rights to immigrants enhances their integration. Large numbers of immigrants have used their voting rights. Parties across the political spectrum now actively look for suitable candidates from immigrant groups in order to attract the immigrant vote. The number of municipal councilors who are non-nationals or of immigrant origin have clearly increased over time. In the Netherlands, even the openly anti-Islam party of Pim Fortuyn made sure it had candidates of immigrant origin on its list for the 2002 national elections.

However, the answer is less clear if one defines integration in normative or emotional terms and cares more about immigrant attitudes than immigrant behavior. If the decisive question is "Have immigrants have become more like us?", then those who vote for candidates of their own immigrant group may not be considered sufficiently integrated. Of course, this voting behaviour may perfectly express an essential element of democracy: every individual can vote for the representative that in his or her personal view will best understand and represent the interests of all voters.

Are immigrants with local voting rights more likely to join political parties, trade unions and other (community) associations than immigrants without voting rights? Cross-country comparative research can best answer this question. Although this type of research is not yet available, a recent Swiss study has compared the political activities of immigrants in Neuchâtel (where they have voting rights) with immigrants in Zürich (where they have none). The first results indicate that having voting rights encourages immigrants to get involved in other political activities (Giugni 2007).

Immigrants who have the right to vote and use it will probably be more active in political parties and other associations; this is similar to the correlation between voting and active citizenship among nationals. The observation of an Irish expert that "the experiences of those who stood for election, as well as those of the electorate which voted for them [was] an invaluable learning experience and a preparation for national politics" (Éinrí 2007), may apply to other European states as well.

In some EU Member States, third-country nationals do not have the right to vote, but they have the right to form associations, establish political parties or become members of an existing party; this is possible in France, Germany, Greece, Italy, Poland and Spain. On the other hand, in Lithuania and Slovenia, long-term resident non-nationals have the right to vote in local elections but not the right to join a political party. Such restrictions will not enhance active citizenship.

Immigrant Political Parties?

The fear that immigrants would establish their own parties has turned out to be largely unfounded. In the Netherlands, some immigrant parties participate in each municipal election, but they rarely obtain enough votes for a seat in the municipal council. Most immigrant politicians and voters apparently see a path to political power through participating in traditional (Dutch) parties or voting for those parties. Ireland presents a striking example: a group of 60 asylum seekers founded a local branch of Fianna Fáil, Ireland's largest political party (Éinrí 2007).

In most countries, immigrants have different homelands and religions, and not all belong to the same social class. This heterogeneity severely reduces the chances of immigrant parties, even in countries with a system of proportional representation. Countries with an electoral system less favorable to small parties (countries in which the candidate with the most votes wins or countries that require a party to have a minimum percentage of all votes), provide an even greater incentive for immigrant voters to vote for and participate in existing political parties. Special immigrant parties under such systems only rarely win a seat in the municipal council.

Influence of Foreign Governments?

Governments of immigrant-origin countries have rarely tried to openly influence the way their nationals or co-ethnics vote. Exceptions to this rule have received quite critical press attention, for example in 1986 when King Hassan of Morocco attempted to influence Moroccan nationals in the Netherlands. The king advised them to abstain from voting in the first municipal elections of the Netherlands in which non-nationals were allowed to participate ("You cannot walk behind two flags"). It was also the first time that a large number of Moroccan nationals could vote in a European country. The king's appeal contributed to a low turnout of Moroccan voters. In later elections, however, King Hassan advised Moroccan immigrants in Europe to use their democratic rights.

Voting Rights and Naturalization

None of the countries with local voting rights have seen naturalization numbers decline. In the Netherlands, the annual number of naturalizations quadrupled from 20,000 in 1986 to 80,000 in 1996, in the decade after the country had granted municipal voting rights.

Most probably, other variables determine the decision to become naturalized. These include the loss or the obligation to give up the original nationality, high fees, difficult language and integration tests, emotional ties to the country of origin or the loss of property and inheritance rights in that country. Immigrants weigh such barriers and disadvantages of citizenship against its perceived advantages, such as visa-free travel, free movement in the European Union, full voting rights and access to public-service jobs reserved for nationals.

In an early 1990s study on why immigrants in the Netherlands decided to become naturalized, two-thirds of those interviewed said that secure legal status and full voting rights were important factors in their decision. Only visa-free travel was mentioned more often (Van den Bedem 1993). Local voting rights, apparently, are not a barrier, but rather function as an incentive to become naturalized. Therefore, policymakers should see local voting rights and naturalization as complementary measures.

Immigrant Political Power Becomes Visible

During the Dutch municipal elections of March 2006, immigrant voters turned out in large numbers to express their discontent with the anti-immigrant politics (personified by the then Immigration and Integration Minister Rita Verdonk) of the center-right government. Press reports and empirical research indicate that the Social Democratic Party won the local elections in Amsterdam and Rotterdam mainly because of immigrant voters, both naturalized and long-term residents. Another consequence: the openly anti-immigrant party in Rotterdam lost its councilors.

The immigrant vote also affected the elections of January 2008 in the German federal state of Hesse. The Christian Democrat leader Roland Koch (CDU) openly played on anti-immigrant sentiments in the final phase of his campaign. His party lost 12 percent of the votes and their overall majority, beating the Social Democratic Party (SPD) by a margin of only 3,500 votes. The eligible Turkish-German electorate in Hesse, estimated at 70,000, could well have decided the outcome in such a close election (*Süddeutsche Zeitung* 29 January 2008 and *Migration und Bevölkerung* February/March 2008: 2).

In both countries, leaders of traditional parties became aware that while anti-immigrant agendas will attract some voters, they cannot discount the importance of immigrant voters either. In the Netherlands, immigrants make up between ten and 15 percent of the electorate; the percentage may be even higher in major cities. In cases where the major parties are almost of the same size, the immigrant vote may decide elections. The outcome of the Dutch municipal elections in 2006 could be considered as proof that granting local voting rights has contributed to immigrants' political integration of immigrants. For those who worry about including immigrants in society, this development may well confirm their worst fears.

Policy Recommendations

1. The European Union should not aim to formally harmonize national voting-rights laws through binding EU law. The European Union has no legal competence with respect to voting rights of third-country nationals. Moreover, any EU action on this issue should respect the cultural, demographic, historical, constitutional and political diversity of the Member States.
2. Harmonization on this issue can only succeed through "soft" methods of coordination, namely through consultations between Member State representatives on the issues of political rights and nationality law, and through the exchange of experiences and recommendations. The issue of nationality law, if only because of its relationship to free movement law, will inevitably appear on the EU agenda. It was already the case at the European Council in Tampere. The Nordic Union model offers a way to reach a consensus.
3. A systematic survey of the available empirical evidence on local voting rights and their effects on the 17 European countries that have already granted these rights could serve as a basis for rational discussion in Europe and elsewhere, including North America.
4. States that do not allow immigrants to vote in local elections would probably need to amend their constitutions to permit such rights. This is a difficult process. States could pass this type of amendment more easily if they package it with more general changes in the constitution.

5. Starting a structured debate on voting and other political rights for immigrants, irrespective of their nationality, could shift the restrictive tone of "integration policy" toward the inclusive principles that have governed the (E)EC since 1957. Secure residence rights and equal treatment encourage immigrants to integrate.

6. States should be discouraged from using reciprocity requirements or agreements because reciprocity places non-nationals' democratic involvement in the hands of (possibly undemocratic) governments in the countries of origin. Moreover, reciprocity results in unequal treatment of resident third-country nationals that is politically hard to justify and that makes states vulnerable to charges of discrimination based on nationality.

7. Restricting voting rights to those with permanent residence status should be avoided because several countries severely restrict access to permanent resident status through strict language and integration tests or grant the status only to certain ethnic groups.

8. States should base voting rights on length of residence in the country and not on the decisions of immigration authorities. Long lawful residence (three to five years) has proved to be an acceptable and easy-to-administer condition; this approach avoids administrative burdens and obstacles as well. Residence is the sole condition, beyond what is required from nationals, that the 1992 Council of Europe convention provides for.

9. Consultations in EU bodies should not be restricted to voting rights, but also cover other political rights of resident third-country nationals, such as the right to join or establish political parties or other associations, trade union rights, access to public service, etc.

10. The EU Council of Ministers should encourage Member States to ratify the 1992 Convention on the Participation of Foreigners in Public Life at the Local Level.

Further Reading

Bedem, van den R.F.A. *Motieven voor naturalisatie.* Arnhem: Gouda Quint (WODC Series no. 125), 1993.

Dubajic, Nénad. Le vote des étrangers au Luxembourg: évolution de 1999 à 2005. *Migrations Société* (XIX) 114: 129–140, 2007.

Éinrí, Piaras Mac. *The recognition of the rights of non-EU citizens to suffrage in local elections in Ireland,* paper presented at the colloquium on "Political participation of aliens at local level", Institut de dret public, Barcelona, 19/20 July 2007.

European Commission. *Report from the Commission to the European Parliament and to the Council on granting a derogation pursuant to Article 19(1) of the EC Treaty,* presented under Article 12(4) of Directive 94/80/EC on the right to vote and stand as a candidate in municipal elections, Brussels, COM(2005) 382.

European Commission. *Communication from the Commission to the European Parliament, the Council, the European Economic and Social Committee and the Committee of the Regions,* Brussels, COM(2007) 780 final.

Geyer, Florian. *Trends in the EU-27 regarding participation of third-country nationals in the host country's political life,* Briefing Paper for the LIBE Commission of the European Parliament, Brussels 2007. www.ipolnet.ep.parl.union.eu/ipolnet/cms.

Giugni, Marco. *Voting Rights for Foreigners in Switzerland,* paper presented at the colloquium on "Political participation of aliens at local level", Institut de dret public, Barcelona, 19/20 July 2007.

Grosso, Enrico. *Aliens and rights of political participation at local level in the Italian constitutional system,* paper presented at the colloquium on "Political participation of aliens at local level", Institut de dret public, Barcelona, 19/20 July 2007.

Jacobs, Dirk. *Nieuwkomers in de politiek, Het parlementaire debat omtrent kiesrecht voor vreemdelingen in Nederland en België,* diss. Utrecht: Academia Press, 1998.

Jacobs, Dirk. The debate over enfranchisement of foreign residents in Belgium. *Journal of Ethnic and Migration Studies* (25) 1999: 649–663.

Jacobs, Dirk. *Local voting rights for non-EU nationals in Belgium*, paper presented at the colloquium on "Political participation of aliens at local level", Institut de dret public, Barcelona, 19/20 July 2007.

Michon, Laure, Jean Tillie and Anaj van Heelsum. *Political participation of immigrants in the Netherlands since 1986*, paper presented at the colloquium on "Political participation of aliens at local level", Institut de dret public, Barcelona, 19/20 July 2007.

Ostergaard-Nielsen, Eva. *Migrants' political rights and participation in Denmark*, paper presented at the colloquium on "Political participation of aliens at local level", Institut de dret public, Barcelona, 19/20 July 2007.

Oriol, Paul. Le droit de vote des résidents étrangers dans l'Union européenne. *Migrations Société* (XIX) 114: 83–98, 2007.

Pastore, Ferruccio. Nationality Law and International Migation: The Italian case. In *Towards a European Nationality, Citizenship, Immigration and Nationality Law in the EU*, edited by Patrick Weil and Randall Hansen. Basingstoke: Palgrave, 2001: 95–117.

Sieveking, Klaus, Klaus Barwig; Klaus Lörchner and Christoph Schumacher (eds.). *Das Kommunalwahlrecht für Ausländer*. Baden-Baden: Nomos Verlag, 1989.

Soininen, Maritta. *30 years of voting rights for immigrants in Swedish local elections—but still not voting*, paper presented at the colloquium on "Political participation of aliens at local level", Institut de dret public, Barcelona, 19/20 July 2007.

Teney, Céline, and Dirk Jacobs. Le droit de vote des étrangers en Belgique: le cas de Bruxelles. *Migrations Société* (XIX) 114: 151–168, 2007.

Waldrauch, Harold. *Electoral rights for foreign nationals: a comparative overview*, paper presented at the ESF workshop on "Citizens, non-citizens and voting rights in Europe", University of Edinburgh, June 2005.

Zibouh, Fatima. Le droit de vote des étrangers aux élections municipale de 2006 en Belgique. *Migrations Société* (XIX) 114: 141–150, 2007.

Dual Citizenship in an Age of Mobility

Thomas Faist, Jürgen Gerdes

In the past, including the recent past, policymakers considered dual citizenship a problem. Leading politicians of previous centuries saw it as an abhorrence of the natural order, the equivalent of bigamy. Citizenship and political loyalty to the state were considered inseparable. Policymakers worried that dual citizens would not integrate into the country to which they had emigrated but rather would maintain exclusive loyalty to the country of original citizenship. And, in times of war in the 19th and early 20th centuries, they feared "foreign" interference by citizens belonging to the enemy. Moreover, democratic legitimacy was at stake. Policymakers feared that dual citizenship would violate the principle "one person, one vote". Also, diplomats were worried that they could not protect their citizens in the country whose citizenship the newly naturalized citizen also held.

Yet, over the last few decades, an astonishing change has taken place: An increasing number of policymakers regard dual citizenship not as a problem for integration, legitimacy, foreign policy and diplomatic protection, but rather as a possibility that needs to be negotiated from various standpoints, ranging from simple pragmatic tolerance to active encouragement. Certainly, dual citizenship is not a completely new phenomenon, but we have witnessed its rapid spread only recently. More than half of all the states in the world, countries of immigration as well as emigration, now tolerate some form or element of dual citizenship (see Figure 1). This policy brief goes beyond statistical trends to the heart of these changes and how best to think through the policy answers.

Whether dual citizenship should be allowed frequently comes up as a question of immigrant integration. Particularly with regard to dual citizenship, integration within and loyalty to a certain nation-state could be perceived as exclusive or viewed in a European (or even global) framework of human, civil and political rights. The answer to the question of whether dual citizenship helps or hinders integration crucially depends on both how one defines integration and how one views the mutual relationship between naturalization and integration.

Viewing integration as exclusive loyalty of immigrants to one state and one state only amounts to a zero-sum game: either one is in or one is out. Such an approach leaves no room for intermediate conditions. By contrast, toleration or even recognition of dual citizenship corresponds with an understanding of integration in the European Union (EU) as a "dynamic two-way process of mutual accommodation by all immigrants and residents of Member States." This is the first of the common basic principles of immigrant integration policy, which the European Council agreed upon in November 2004. Citizenship of the residence state provides immigrants with a voice on an equal basis with native-born citizens. If the "participation of immigrants in the democratic process and in the formulation of integration policies and measures (...) supports their integration", as argued and laid down as another common basic principle on immigrant integration of the European Council, full political inclusion of immigrants is a paramount goal (Commission of the European Communities 2003). The Conclusions of the German Presidency added that general integration policies need to be adopted by all Member States.[1]

This policy brief advocates, in line with EU principles on immigrant integration, that the toleration of dual citizenship can be a tool to promote naturalization. In essence, it is an instrument to close the gap between the resident and the voting populations. Those who are subject to the law should at least have the opportunity to participate in the decision-making process by means of democratic rights. There

1   287th Council Meeting, Justice and Home Affairs, Luxemburg, 12–13 June 2007.

are only two ways of achieving this outcome: by granting the same political rights to immigrant residents—for example, the right to vote on the national level—or by further liberalizing naturalization procedures. One of the major instruments for naturalization is dual citizenship.

Figure 1: Restriction and tolerance towards dual citizenship around the world

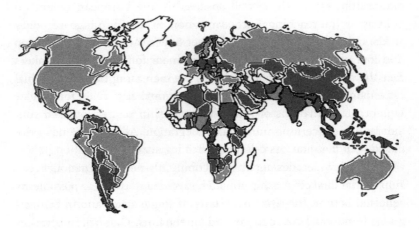

■ Dark-gray is restrictive
■ Light-gray is tolerant

Note: See Annex B for a country list and definition of terms.
Source: Author's depiction, based on United States Office of Personnel Management, Investigations Service, "Citizenship Laws of the World", http://opm.gov/extra/investigate/IS-01.pdf.

Defining Dual Citizenship

Dual citizenship means that individuals combine citizenship in and of two nation-states. In principle, individuals may hold even more than two citizenships; hence the terms "multiple" or "plural" citizenship.

International law stipulates that, as a matter of each nation-state's sovereignty, it determines its citizens according to its own law. The only conditions for international recognition of citizenship are that a so-called genuine link exists between the state citizen and the respective state, and that the self-determination of other states is likewise respected. Further restrictions may arise only out of international agreements.

How widely accepted the principle of nation-state sovereignty in citizenship law is can be well observed in the European Union. In contrast to far-reaching Europeanization in a wide range of policy fields, only the individual EU Member States can decide on access to and loss of state citizenship. In the immediate future, policymakers face the problem of how to deal with the increasing tolerance of dual citizenship that is embedded in international law: rules for gender equality; combinations of rules for citizenship acquisition; and considerations concerning immigrant integration. All of the trends associated with these factors call for explicit legislation.

Until a few decades ago, it was commonly held international consensus that dual citizenship should be avoided as much as possible, as reflected both in the citizenship laws of single states and in bilateral and international conventions and agreements. One brief statement by the League of Nations in 1930 summarizes the dominant international perspective throughout most of the 20th century: "All persons are entitled to possess one nationality, but one nationality only."

States regarded dual citizenship as a potential catalyst for treason, espionage and other subversive activities. From the mid-19th century until long after World War II, states adhered to two iron laws. The first was that losing one's original citizenship was the price for adopting another. Most states expatriated their citizens automatically when they became naturalized in another state; but they also expatriated them if there was significant evidence of political or social loyalty to another state, such as entry into military service or the assumption of a political office in the other state or even participation in political elections abroad. In some cases, immigration countries made naturalization conditional on the relinquishment of the previous citizenship.

The second iron law by which many states attempted to overcome the problem of dual citizenship ensuing from birth in their territory was that such individuals, on reaching maturity, had to choose one of the two citizenships or they were otherwise expatriated.

What changed? Dual citizenship usually arises whenever a person is born within the territory of a country where the law of territoriality *(jus soli)* holds, but whose parents are citizens of a country that observes the blood principle *(jus sanguinis)*. Here, developments in gender equality under the citizenship law were the main legal mechanism for expanding dual citizenship. Previously, the citizenship status of women had entirely depended on their husbands as they automatically acquired their husbands' citizenship upon marriage. The right to retain their own citizenship, independently of their husbands, has been taken up in the citizenship laws of a growing number of countries. At the same time, naturalization for female spouses has become easier so as to afford better protection to families. For example, it is frequently the case that a child can be given the citizenship of either parent. All the 15 long-standing EU Member States (EU-15[2]) accept the dual citizenship of children of mixed-nationality marriages. However, in cases of binational children born out of wedlock, the Scandinavian countries, Austria and the Netherlands still impose some restrictions regarding transmission of the father's citizenship.

Furthermore, in recent years, European immigration countries have increasingly made naturalization less conditional on the relinquishment of previous citizenship, as reflected in changes to national citizenship laws, relaxation of administrative practices and more generous interpretations of international agreements. For the most part, governments have regarded easing citizenship acquisition as beneficial for immigrant integration and as a requirement of democratic legitimacy.

Legislative changes have facilitated citizenship acquisition for the children of immigrants (also known as "the second generation") in

---

2   The EU-15 encompasses Austria, Belgium, Denmark, Finland, France, Germany, Greece, Ireland, Italy, Luxemburg, Netherlands, Portugal, Spain, Sweden and the United Kingdom.

several ways. These include introducing some form of *jus soli* or rights to opt into citizenship at maturity, a reduction of naturalization requirements for first-generation immigrants and an increasing acceptance of dual citizenship. With regard to citizenship acquisition by *jus soli* or simple declaration of the second generation, the result of dual citizenship is usually accepted. An exception is Germany, which requires *jus soli* citizens to opt for one of their citizenships at maturity.

Among the EU-15, only six still require renunciation of previous citizenship. Spain, however, does not require proof of the actual loss of previous citizenship although the law mandates it. In the Netherlands, Germany, Austria, Denmark and Luxembourg, the renunciation requirement has a number of exceptions. For instance, all these countries allow dual citizenship when renunciations are legally impossible or extremely difficult, and individuals with recognized refugee status may also have dual citizenship. In the Netherlands, Germany and Denmark, these and other exceptions result in dual citizenships in 40 to 50 percent of all naturalization cases.

However, the ten states that joined the European Union in 2004 are less tolerant towards dual citizenship in cases of naturalization. Only three states—Cyprus, Hungary and Malta—explicitly accept dual citizenship of immigrants. Remarkably, six of the remaining states are countries that only recently became independent: the Baltic states (Estonia, Latvia and Lithuania), the Czech Republic, Slovakia and Slovenia.

In European countries that do not belong to the European Union, the situation also varies. For example, Switzerland has tolerated dual citizenship of immigrants since the early 1990s. Norway requires individuals to renounce their previous citizenship before they can become Norwegian citizens.

The growing tolerance towards dual citizenship has also strengthened the rights of expatriates. In the past, they were mostly excluded from political participation in their countries of origin. Currently, extraterritorial voting rights for citizens living abroad are widespread. In some cases, external voting may even have an impact on national elections, as it did in Italy in 2006.

Emigration countries are also confronted with the problem of whether, and under what conditions, their citizens living abroad can retain or lose their citizenship.

Among European countries, policies have moved toward accepting dual citizenship. In 1973, French citizens were no longer required to give up their citizenship if they became naturalized in another state. Portugal implemented a similar law in 1981, Italy in 1992, Sweden in 2001, and Finland in 2003. In some European states, such as Italy, Sweden and Finland, the desire of emigrants to retain their nationality played an important role in the decisions of the respective governments to accept the dual citizenship of immigrants.

Countries outside Europe have also eased restrictions on emigrants who become naturalized. Many allow emigrants to retain their citizenship, make it easier for them to regain their citizenship or have mitigated the consequences of losing citizenship. These include emigration countries such as Turkey, India, Tunisia, Mexico, El Salvador, Colombia and the Dominican Republic. Some of these countries do not allow their emigrants full dual citizenship. Instead they offer a sort of 'light citizenship'. For example, in the early 1980s, the Turkish government passed a law that guaranteed Turkish-born emigrants (who have acquired the citizenship of the state in which they reside) the same rights as Turkish citizens on a number of issues such as pensions and property. Since the mid-1990s Turkish citizens who naturalize in Germany can hold a 'pink card', which granted card holders rights equal to those held by full Turkish citizens, except the right to vote in Turkish elections.

These changing policies and attitudes toward dual citizenship originated in international law. The European Convention on the Reduction of Cases of Dual Nationality and Military Obligations in Cases of Dual Nationality of 1963 still clearly aimed at limiting the instances of dual citizenship. However, the 1997 European Convention on Nationality, which the overwhelming majority of European states have signed, contains no provision referring to dual citizenship as an abnormality that needs to be eliminated. Instead, the 1997 Convention expands the discretion of the contracting states to tolerate dual citizenship. It also provides for explicit acceptance when children acquire dual citizenship by birth and when renunciation or loss is not possible or cannot reasonably be required. The European Convention on Nationality, together with other developments in international law, illustrate an increasing trend toward recognizing citizenship as a human right, including the right to citizenship of the state in which individuals permanently reside.

Although it is likely that the number of dual citizens has risen consistently over the past decades, it is difficult to provide reliable estimates. States usually register only their own citizens and do not count the number of citizenships acquired. Moreover, people with two or more citizenships may keep quiet to avoid administrative difficulties. Germany is one of the few countries which counts dual citizens in cases of naturalization. According to the newsletter *Migration und Bevölkerung* (2006), about 45 percent of all naturalizations between 2000 and 2006 involved new citizens who were allowed to keep their original citizenship. If one is interested in the total number of dual citizens residing in German territory, then dual citizenships arising from other instances, such as children of binational couples, have to be added. How difficult it is to assess the total number of dual citizens can also be seen in related efforts in the United States, where, for example, estimates range from 500,000 to 5.7 million US dual citizens (Renshon 2001).

In sum, the two most important factors explaining the increasing tolerance toward dual citizenship are: first, the changing relationships between individual nation states; and second, altered relations between states and citizens. Dual citizenship can be seen as a result of nation state politics. While previous bilateral and multilateral forms of international cooperation aimed to avoid instances of dual and multiple citizenships, more and more nation states have opted out of this interpretation. Interstate cooperation concerning nationality acquisition was regarded as necessary in the 19th century for enforcing the principle of one citizenship against competing military conscription claims of other states. This necessity no longer exists. Many European states have abolished mandatory military service. For those states that still have conscription, the dominant principle is that dual citizens are obliged to perform military service in the state of residence and are exempt from military service in the state of their other citizenship. Consequently, pressures on nation-states to cooperate in avoiding dual citizenship have decreased significantly while the leeway to pursue national interests through national citizenship laws has expanded.

In parallel, enhanced economic and political cooperation between democratic nation states, the creation of the European Union, the end of the Cold War and, especially, the decreasing probability of interstate wars between democracies has meant that nation-states are becoming less and less concerned about their citizens' loyalty.

The growing importance of human rights norms has also helped the rise of dual citizenship. These norms have limited state discretion. Liberal democratic states, even when adhering to the principle of avoiding dual citizenship as far as possible, are compelled to grant at least certain exemptions. This tendency is linked to principles of legitimacy in democratic political systems. For instance, liberal democracies accept dual citizenship upon naturalization if the other state makes renouncing citizenship impossible or imposes unreasonable demands. Liberal democratic states also tend to accept dual citizenship in the name of gender equality when citizenship is acquired by birth. Furthermore, such states may be inclined to grant dual citizenship on the basis of reciprocity within regional governance systems, such as the European Union.

So far, policymakers have responded explicitly by passing new citizenship laws but also by abstaining from regulation and thus implicit toleration. Yet integration in the European Union, based on the common principles of integration, demands more explicit coordination.

The Benefits of Dual Citizenship

Given the trend toward dual citizenship and the need for a common EU integration policy, liberal democracies are faced with deleterious consequences if they host large numbers of immigrants without granting them access to full rights and responsibilities. The dominant trend of conceiving citizenship acquisition as a means of immigrant integration has led to the liberalization and de-ethnicization of citizenship laws. Consequently, naturalization has become easier, and more countries tolerate dual citizenship. Accordingly, citizenship laws from the 1980s to 2005 in the EU-15 became more liberal.

Taking three significant indicators—birthright citizenship *(jus soli)* for the children of immigrants, the length of residence required for naturalization and the tolerance of dual citizenship—it turns out that Germany, Luxembourg, Finland, Sweden and the Netherlands have significantly liberalized naturalization requirements. The rules for citizenship acquisition in these five countries converged with those of the remaining ten long-standing EU Member States. The growing liberalization in general and the toleration of dual citizenship in particular has yielded a number of specific benefits:

Dual Citizenship as a Means to Increase Naturalization Rates

Not all immigrants who are eligible to acquire citizenship actually submit an application. Although the reasons why immigrants become naturalized depend on a number of factors, there are strong indications that the requirement to renounce their previous citizenship is one of the most important obstacles. For instance, whereas the naturalization rates of Turkish immigrants in the Netherlands rose sharply between 1992 and 1997 (the period when dual citizenship was tolerated without exceptions), an equivalent group of Turkish immigrants in neighboring Germany (which, as a general rule, did not accept dual citizenship) had much lower naturalization rates.

Similar results can be observed in North America. Immigrants in Canada are more inclined to become naturalized than are those in the United States. One of the reasons is simple: The United States still demands a renunciation of prior citizenship during the naturalization procedure. Though immigrants tend to know that the United

States will not take action against those holding another citizenship, the renunciation requirement implies that the country will not tolerate dual citizenship. This approach contrasts with Canada, where dual citizenship is valorized in official government statements. The Canadian situation can be seen as an expression of the "ethnic paradox". The ethnicity paradox holds that attachment to ethnic origins actually helps group members to become incorporated into the host polity.

In Europe, data compiled by the Organization for Economic Cooperation and Development (OECD) in 2007 showed that easing the retention of original citizenship—with all other factors held equal, such as residence requirements and restrictive or liberal administrative practices—led to increased naturalization rates between 1996 and 2005. Those countries that did not tolerate the retention of original citizenship had lower naturalization rates. For example, the rates in Germany, Spain, Luxembourg and the Czech Republic were lower than in Sweden, Switzerland or the United Kingdom. Since 2000, average acquisition rates have ranged from 2.1 percent in Germany to 7.6 percent in Sweden, with the other four states taking the middle ground of approximately 4 to 5.5 percent. Some countries, such as Portugal and Italy, which accept dual citizenship, have rather low rates of immigrant naturalization. In these cases, however, permanent residents must wait for long periods before they can become naturalized.

Political participation is highly valued among many dual citizens, especially in countries such as Portugal, Germany, and the United Kingdom. However, in the United Kingdom, many non-citizens reported they were not dissatisfied that they could not vote, but, at the same time, they felt a lack of representation (Pitkänen and Kalekin-Fishman 2007). This refers to an important aspect of the congruence between the rulers and the ruled that is independent of actual political participation. Although non-citizen immigrants usually have wide opportunities for political participation, such as forming political associations, they are not represented in a very important sense. If they lack the right to vote, it is likely that political representatives and those running for political office will not take the concerns of these non-citizen immigrants seriously because they cannot expect votes from them.

Dual Citizenship Advances Overall Participation

Although it depends on the legal framework of the host country in which an immigrant is residing, holding citizenship of that country, in many cases, avoids the need for a work permit, entails full protection against expulsion, enables access to public employment, decreases administrative difficulties and, in the EU context, allows for mobility within the European Union without a visa. Such advantages tied to citizenship will clearly enhance the probability of socioeconomic integration.

Dual Citizenship Enhances Transnational Participation beyond the European Union

In particular, the freedom to travel across borders, greater labor-market opportunities and access to educational institutions are advantages often mentioned by immigrants in Estonia, Finland, France, Germany and Portugal (Pitkänen and Kalekin-Fishman 2007). Concerning their country of origin, immigrants may enjoy privileged access to the territory and the economic sector, for example by retaining inheritance and property rights. Without dual citizenship—and statuses similar to it, such as Turkey's Pink Card—such privileges may be otherwise lost.

In the destination country, the acceptance of dual citizenship recognizes the specific symbolic and emotional ties that immigrants have; it also gives them an opportunity to choose their own integration course. Interestingly, transnational participation may also be beneficial for national integration. This corresponds to the empirically substantiated finding that not all immigrants experience a uniform path of integration (Faist 2000).

In Europe, some immigrants assimilate culturally and gradually lose their ties to regions of origin; others maintain ties to regions of origin and destination over several generations.

A third category of immigrants includes those who engage globally in this era of increased mobility of people, information, money and consumer goods. Especially in countries with a high proportion of immigrants, networks, groups and organizations have emerged that connect people in many different places. These "transnational social spaces", understood as combinations of social and symbolic ties, networks and organizations and networks of organizations that reach across the borders of multiple states, allow for and often facilitate certain types of incorporation. For example, the immigrant entrepreneur who needs to mobilize contacts across borders could benefit by retaining the citizenship of his home country.

Dual Citizenship Enhances Esteem and Self-Respect

Many migrants commonly have attachments and involvements in two or more places across nation-state borders; consequently they have plural identifications and loyalties. When dual citizens regard their citizenships as essential to their identity, deciding which citizenship they would keep if they had to give one up could cause emotional difficulties. These dual citizens regard the state's acceptance of dual citizenship as a kind of official legitimization of their multicultural identity. In this sense, dual citizenship can be regarded as symbolically acknowledging transnational living circumstances, such as growing up within different cultural and ethnic backgrounds, nations and religions; in this respect dual citizenship can promote the integration process.

In particular, children can be integrated more easily if the respective state accepts or even welcomes dual citizenship. This is mainly because the state is likely to encourage such children to develop specific competencies related to a transnational background, such as bilingualism and intercultural mediation. In Germany, for example, children of binational marriages, who are dual citizens from birth, regard their dual citizenship as important for their integration (Schröter and Jäger 2007).

Within local contexts of participation and intercultural contacts, dual citizenship may also help natives recognize immigrants as full and equal members of society. Although discrimination takes many forms, the distinction between aliens and citizens also plays a certain role in situations of disrespect. Citizenship status may help immigrants to see themselves as competent members of society and worthy of respect from others.

These considerations are relevant for further developing more recent notions of "civic citizenship", as the European Commission and European Parliament emphasized (Commission of the European Communities 2003). Civic citizenship aims to enhance mutual tolerance, solidarity and trust between migrants and citizens. Since civic citizenship does not mandate that all those included are full citizens, dual citizens, with their bicultural competences, may play a particularly important role as mediators between citizens and newcomers. (For a summary, see Table 1.)

Table 1: The contribution of dual citizenship to immigrant integration

Dimensions of citizenship rights	Citizenship acquisition of the immigration state	Retaining original citizenship
Belonging and membership	Full legal membership, which may contribute to acceptance of immigrants on the part of the indigenous population and may help immigrants identify with the state of residence	Recognition of transnational ties and related multicultural skills
Pragmatic benefits	Avoidance of visa requirements, and easier access to education and (public) employment in the state of residence as well as in EU countries	Preservation of rights connected to citizenship (e.g., privileged access to territory, inheritance and property rights, entitlement to trade registering), which may be beneficial for strategies of economic subsistence

Problems Dual Citizenship Poses

Despite the benefits of dual citizenship, some countries resist the increasing tolerance towards it because of fears about the consequences of dual voting, of a lack of integration and loyalty, and of a devaluation of citizenship. These worries need to be taken seriously.

Dual Voting

A question that often comes up in public debates is the problem of dual voting rights. In Sweden, the potential violation of the principle of "one person, one vote" was what opponents of liberalizing citizenship laws regarded as the most important problem. However, the benefit of having more people participating in the state where they reside was later seen as outweighing the problem of double voting.

Moreover, the problem is overestimated: Even if voting rights are exercised in two or more countries, the votes are usually aggregated in different elections and polities and therefore do not count twice. This is important because many European states allow emigrants, under certain conditions, to vote at the national level. For example, among the EU-15 Member States, only Greece and Ireland do not grant voting rights to citizens residing abroad. Since equal-treatment clauses usually prohibit different treatment of emigrants with single citizenship and those with dual citizenship, dual citizens residing abroad usually have voting rights. If links between the respective citizens and states continue to exist, it seems obvious as well as legitimate that these ties should be governed by democratic procedures. However, if a citizen of both Germany and France were allowed to vote in each country for the European Parliament, this would mean her vote would be counted twice. This would clearly violate the principle of "one person, one vote".

In answer to the objection that dual citizens are privileged because they can pursue their interests by casting ballots in two separate polities, one can argue that people with more money and other resources exert a larger influence in elections than others do. This is different in federal political systems, such as the United States or Germany, or proto-federal systems, such as the European Union.

Lack of Integration

Two broader issues support the view that integration should be proved and tested. The first refers to alleged patterns of failed integration, with reference to immigrants' high unemployment rates together with their lower educational levels and their higher-than-average dependence on welfare.

The second issue concerns a growing fear of Islamic fundamentalism and terrorism, which has led to an increased political and public observance of illiberal traditional and religious practices in some European countries; these practices include headscarf wearing, forced and arranged marriages and honor killings. Worries about immigrants from Muslim countries increased in the aftermath of September 11 and the bombings in Madrid and London, among other events.

However, while empirical evidence suggests dual citizenship may increase political participation and socioeconomic opportunities, there is no plausible argument, and indeed no proof, that dual citizenship contributes to spirals of non-integration, exclusion and segregation.

Lack of Loyalty

Citizenship implies that an individual identifies with common political values, a sense of responsibility toward the common good and a sense of solidarity with fellow citizens in a particular nation-state. For governments, the most pressing problem regarding loyalty concerns those permanent residents who are not willing to renounce their citizenship of origin. There may be people who have been permanent residents of a country for many years without ever wanting to acquire the citizenship of that country.

Immigrants who maintain social and symbolic ties to their home countries, as expressed in their wish to retain their original citizenship, are often seen by the dominant groups in immigration societies as lacking substantive identification with their country of settlement. After all, many of them probably will not return to the country of origin or engage in onward migration. It is hard to believe integration as well as their loyalty to the state of residence will be enhanced under such conditions. Consequently, it has been suggested by proponents of dual citizenship that those states with low naturalization rates could take a more pragmatic view of dual citizenship.

The Devaluation of National Citizenship

Dual citizenship is connected to the fear that national citizenship will lose its value. There is also no consensus on whether citizenship acquisition is a prerequisite for integration or the crowning of a process. Current policy innovations and changes suggest that the latter perspective is gaining prominence as states have begun to introduce naturalization and other tests and requirements. All of these are in response to the fear of non-integration and even perceived integration failures attributed to immigrants' behavior. Many European states, including those that have long viewed citizenship as a means of integration, such as the Netherlands, have introduced stricter language and integration requirements as a precondition for acquiring residence permits and citizenship. Migrants who fail to meet these requirements could face sanctions. A growing number of European states have established citizenship tests—a longstanding practice in the United States and Canada—with corresponding formal exams to test language skills and knowledge of society. These states include Denmark in 2002, France and the Netherlands in 2003, Greece in 2004, the United Kingdom in 2005 and, most recently, Austria and some German federal states (Länder) in 2006.

The idea underlying "naturalization as the crowning of a completed integration process" is that citizenship laws should specify reliable criteria for comprehensive and successful socioeconomic and civic integration. This means that immigrants need to fulfill these criteria before acquiring citizenship and the full spectrum of individual rights connected with it. Making acquisition dependent on individual performance extends beyond immigration and naturalization policies. For example, certain welfare rights are increasingly based on citizens first agreeing to conform to state-defined appropriate behavior. These measures, as well as increased attention to criteria such as income and other economic qualifications, must be seen as a defense of national citizenship.

This shift, which, at first glance, is only a sign of a more restrictive approach toward citizenship, comes partly from EU Member States' fear that expanding European citizenship devalues national citizenship. Countries have relaxed the requirements for acquiring citizenship, embraced dual citizenship and made territorial birthright citizenship the norm—developments that all seem irreversible.

At the root is a perceived trade-off between national citizenship (embodying territorial assumptions of full membership) and European citizenship (consisting mostly of individual rights of personhood, such as human rights or rights of residence). This tension is hard to resolve.

At stake is a new balance between legal citizenship—often called "nationality"—and political citizenship. Political citizenship consists of three mutually interacting dimensions: equal political liberty, reciprocal rights and obligations between states and citizens, and collective affiliation to a political community. Rights and obligations have been partially decoupled from legal nationality, and collective affiliation can refer to several nations in the case of dual citizenship or even supranations, as in European Union citizenship. Yet the common root of citizenship is still the same, whether we talk of national, dual or European Union citizenship, namely equal political freedom. Thus, it is important to remember that the political concept of citizenship does not only consist of rights and obligations and affiliation to national identity, but also includes the idea that people subject to laws are also their authors.

Future Implications of Dual Citizenship

The inevitability of dual or plural citizenship suggests that states should welcome dual citizenship. Arguments against it are weak. First, the fear of dual voting is misplaced because—if at all—migrants vote in different nation-states. Second, the spread of dual citizenship has obviously not led to a noticeable increase in interstate tensions and conflicts. The problems of conflicting laws, rights and duties regarding taxation, family rights, military service and inheritance can be solved by referring to the state of habitual residence and/or through bilateral or multilateral treaties. Third, even if one has doubts about the loyalty of dual citizens, it is better to have them as citizens than non-citizens.

The evidence suggests that policymakers should not only tolerate dual citizenship but also support it. First, dual citizenship leads to higher rates of naturalization and thus encourages overall social and political integration. Second, dual citizenship enhances democratic legitimacy because it embraces both the resident immigrant population and the rest of the general population. Third, on balance, and with the definitional caveats such a statement will inevitably provoke, dual citizenship promotes integration—regardless of whether the citizenship regime seeks to integrate immigrants or to crown the process of integration. But for policymakers grappling with this issue, there is an equally sound reason: it is pragmatic, efficient and more cost-effective to recognize dual citizenship, and to otherwise allocate resources towards improving other aspects of the integration process. Fourth, dual citizenship transcends exclusive either-or notions and rules of membership in political communities. The increasing toleration of dual citizenship in Europe and around the globe reflects life across borders and multiple belonging.

In effect, the spread of dual citizenship helps to further overcome dichotomies between concepts of immigrant incorporation. Migrants generally do not cut ties to their countries of origin right away. This observation needs to be complemented: Since one of the major functions of dual citizenship is to prepare immigrants for incorporation into the country of settlement, dual citizenship could be temporary because the salience of the original citizenship might, in some cases, decline over the course of time. In a mobile world, dual citizenship will nonetheless continue to grow as new immigrants and their children strive to become full members of liberal democratic communities.

Policy Recommendations

1. Accept dual citizenship as a rule. In order to participate in public life and politics, education and employment, as laid down by the common EU principles of integration, citizenship of both the host and origin countries usually benefits migrants. It allows them to integrate into the country of immigration and to maintain their rights in the country of origin. The fear of citizenship being devalued is largely misplaced since, for most immigrants, instrumental and symbolic factors are interwoven.

2. Strengthen harmonization trends in the European Union. EU Member States should tolerate dual citizenship so that immigrants in all Member States are not subjected to severe or unequal treatment regarding the conditions of naturalization. Because most EU Member States tolerate dual citizenship, they have already set the stage for harmonization. In this way, dual citizenship can serve as a link between national citizenship and EU citizenship.

3. Make dual citizenship part of citizenship education. Because of renewed discussions about the importance of national citizenship and a concern among Member States that citizenship might become devalued, the EU concept of civic citizenship needs to be part of citizenship education in schools and other institutions of learning. Civic citizenship implies participation in public life. It embraces both (multiple) national, local and supranational forms of citizenship, and thus goes to the root of citizenship, namely democracy.

4. Widen the scope of citizenship ceremonies. In an age of mobility and the growing importance of international norms, dual citizen-

ship can more effectively advance civil and political engagement than simply extending rights to non-citizens. Therefore, policymakers should embrace dual citizenship and institute citizenship ceremonies that reflect the importance of belonging and integration.

5. Make dual citizens part of development and peace cooperation. Immigrants who are well-integrated into the country of immigration can mediate across borders. Under certain circumstances, dual citizens can take part in development cooperation and conflict mediation. The children of immigrants are especially well-positioned to act as conflict mediators since they are less likely to be actively involved in the conflicts.

Annex A: Research on Dual Citizenship

Dual citizenship has entered the research agenda of the social and political sciences only very recently. So far, most studies have been concerned with the perspective of nation-states, pertaining to policies of immigrant integration and citizenship law in general (e.g., Bauböck et al. 2006) and the development of international law (e.g., Chan 1991; Spiro 1997; Koslowski 2003). Related empirical research has focused either on single countries (e.g., Renshon 2001) or on comparisons of more or less different states (e.g., Aleinikoff and Klusmeyer 2001 and 2002; Martin and Hailbronner 2003; Hansen and Weil 2001; Howard 2005; Faist 2007; Kalekin-Fishman and Pitkänen 2007). Only a few empirical studies explore dual citizenship from the migrant's perspective, that is, their incentives for acquiring dual citizenship and their motives for keeping it, and their use of opportunities connected to "dual" citizenship rights in US and Canadian contexts (e.g., Bloemraad 2007), as well as in selected European countries (Pitkänen and Kalekin-Fishman 2007). Even fewer studies draw attention to the nexus between citizenship, cross-border engagement of immigrants (Faist and Özveren 2004) and the implications these have for integration (Faist 2000) or to the implications of dual citizenship for overall citizenship and societal integration (Kivisto and Faist 2007; Spiro 2007).

Annex B: Country Laws

Europe

Tolerant	Restrictive
Bulgaria	Andorra (3)
Federal Republic of Yugoslavia	Austria (4)
Sweden	Belgium (4)
Cyprus	Croatia
France	Czech Republic (3)
Greece	Denmark (3, 4)
Switzerland	Finland (2,3,4,)
Serbia and Montenegro	Germany (2,3,4)
Hungary	Iceland
Ireland	Netherlands (3, 4)
Italy	Norway (3, 4)
Latvia	Poland (3)
Portugal	Romania
Lithuania	Ukraine
Macedonia	
Malta	
Spain (only in certain cases)	
Turkey	
United Kingdom	

Americas

Tolerant	Restrictive
Antigua and Barbuda	Argentina (except for Spanish citizens) (4)
Barbados	Bahamas
Belize	Bolivia
Brazil (3)	Chile (2, 3, 4)
Canada	Cuba (3)
Chile (only in certain cases)	Dominican Republic (2, 3, 4)
Colombia (3)	Ecuador (except for Spanish citizens) (3, 4)
Costa Rica	Venezuela (2, 3, 4)
El Salvador	
Mexico	
Peru	
United States of America	

Africa

Tolerant	Restrictive
Benin	Algeria (4)
Burkina Faso	Angola (2, 4)
Cape Verde	Botswana (2, 3, 4)
Central African Republic	Burundi (3, 4)
Egypt	Cameroon (3, 4)
Nigeria	Congo (3, 4)
Mauritius	Djibouti (3, 4)
South Africa	Ghana
	Kenya (2, 3, 4)
	Namibia (2, 3, 4)
	Tanzania (2, 3, 4)
	Zimbabwe

Asia and Oceania

Tolerant	Restrictive
Australia	Afghanistan (1, 3, 4)
Bangladesh (only in certain cases)	Armenia (3, 4)
Cambodia	Azerbaijan
Israel	Bahrain
Jordan	Belarus
Lebanon	Bhutan
New Zealand	Brunei (2, 3, 4)
Pakistan	Burma
Russia	China (3)
Syria	Fiji (2, 3, 4)
Tonga (only in certain cases)	India (3, 4)
Western Samoa	Indonesia (3, 4)
	Iran (1)
	Japan (2, 3, 4)
	Kiribati (3)
	Korea North (1)
	Malaysia (3, 4)
	Nepal (3, 4)
	Papua New Guinea (2, 3, 4)
	Philippines (2, 3, 4)
	Singapore (2, 3, 4)
	Solomon Islands (2, 3, 4)
	Thailand (2, 3, 4)
	Vietnam (1, 3)

Source: United States Office of Personnel Management, Investigations Service, "Citizenship Laws of the World", http://opm.gov/extra/investigate/IS-01.pdf.
Note: The most restrictive cases are characterized by the following criteria:
1. Assignment by birth: only one citizenship possible.
2. Obligation to choose one citizenship on reaching maturity.
3. Renunciation requirement (in some cases proof also required) upon naturalization in another country.
4. Forced expatriation upon naturalization in another country.

The more strictly the acquisition of a citizenship is governed by principles (1) to (4), the more restrictive the regime. Conversely, the more lenient the procedure, or the more exemptions from these requirements allowed, the more tolerant the regime.

Further Reading

Aleinikoff, T. Alexander, and Douglas B. Klusmeyer. Plural Nationality: Facing the Future in a Migratory World, In *Citizenship Today.
Global Perspectives and Practices*, edited by T. Alexander Aleinikoff
and Douglas B. Klusmeyer. Washington, DC: Carnegie Endowment
for International Peace, 2001: 63–88.

Aleinikoff, T. Alexander, and Douglas B. Klusmeyer. *Citizenship Policies for an Age of Migration*, Washington, DC: Carnegie Endowment
for International Peace, 2002.

Bauböck, Rainer, Eva. Ersbøll, Kees Groenendijk, and Harald Waldrauch (eds.) *Acquisition and Loss of Nationality: Policies and Trends
in 15 European States*. Vienna: Institute for European Integration
Research, 2006.

Bloemraad, Irene. Much Ado about Nothing? The Contours of Dual
Citizenship in the United States and Canada. In *Dual Citizenship
in Global Perspective: From Unitary to Multiple Citizenship*, edited by
Thomas Faist and Peter Kivisto. Houndmills, UK: Palgrave Macmillan, 2007: 159–186.

Chan, Johannes M. M. The Right to a Nationality as a Human Right.
The Current Trend towards Recognition. *Human Rights Law Journal* 12 (1): 1–14. 1991.

Commission of the European Communities. *On Immigration, Integration and Employment*, (COM (2003) 336 final), June 3, 2003, http://
ec.europa.eu/justice_home/funding/2004_2007/doc/com_2003_
336_final.pdf.

Faist, Thomas. *The Volume and Dynamics of International Migration and
Transnational Social Spaces*. Oxford: Oxford University Press, 2000.

Faist, Thomas, and Eyüp Özveren. *Transnational Social Spaces: Agents,
Networks and Institutions*. Aldershot: Ashgate, 2004.

Faist, Thomas (ed.). *Dual Citizenship in Europe: From Nationhood to
Societal Integration*. Aldershot: Ashgate, 2007.

Faist, Thomas, and Peter Kivisto. *Dual Citizenship in Global Perspective: From Unitary to Multiple Citizenship*. Houndmills, UK: Palgrave Macmillan, 2007.

Hansen, Randall, and Patrick Weil (eds.). *Towards a European Nationality. Citizenship, Immigration and Nationality Law in the EU.* Houndmills, Basingstoke: Palgrave Macmillan, 2001.

Howard, Marc Morjé. Variation in Dual Citizenship Policies in the Countries of the EU. *International Migration Review* 39: 697–720, 2005.

Kalekin-Fishman, Devorah, and Pirkko Pitkänen (eds.). *Multiple Citizenship as a Challenge to European Nation-States.* Rotterdam: Sense Publishers, 2007.

Kivisto, Peter, and Thomas Faist. *Citizenship: Discourse, Theory and Transnational Prospects.* Oxford: Blackwell, 2007.

Koslowski, Rey. Challenges of International Cooperation in a World of Increasing Dual Nationality. In *Rights and Duties of Dual Nationals: Evolution and Prospects,* edited by David Martin and Kay Hailbronner. The Hague: Kluwer Publishers. 2003: 157–182.

Martin, David, and Kay Hailbronner (eds.). *Rights and Duties of Dual Nationals: Evolution and Prospects.* The Hague: Kluwer Publishers, 2003.

Pitkänen, P. Pirkko, and Devorah Kalekin-Fishman (eds.). *Multiple State Membership and Citizenship in an Era of Transnational Migration.* Rotterdam: Sense Publishers, 2007.

Renshon, Stanley A. *Dual Citizenship and American National Identity.* Washington, D.C.: Center for Immigration Studies, 2001.

Schröter, Yvonne, and Reinhold S. Jäger. "We are children of Europe—Multiple citizenship in Germany". In *Multiple State Membership and Citizenship in the Era of Transnational Migration,* edited by Pirkko P. Pitkänen and Devorah Kalekin-Fishman. Rotterdam: Sense Publishers 2007: 67–90.

SOPEMI. *International Migration Outlook.* Paris: OECD—Organisation for Economic Co-operation and Development, 2007.

Spiro, Peter J. Dual Nationality and the Meaning of Citizenship. *Emory Law Review* 46: 1411–1485. 1997.

Spiro, Peter J. *Beyond Citizenship: American Identity After Globalization.* New York: Oxford University Press, 2007.

A New Citizenship Bargain for the Age of Mobility? Citizenship Requirements in Europe and North America

Randall A. Hansen

Citizenship has multiple meanings. For some (Hansen and Weil 2001), it requires the possession of a national passport. For others (Bosniak 2006), it is a "practice" involving multiple forms of political participation: street protests, mail-in campaigns and other forms of direct action that demand the recognition of particular interests. For still others (Carens 2000; Kymlicka 2001), it is a normative question of how people should acquire citizenship and what it should give them. If there is a danger in the current scholarly literature, it is palpably not that there is too little interest in citizenship; rather, that there is too much, and the content of the concept will be stretched to the point where it is almost meaningless.[1]

For the purposes of this overview, citizenship is understood in a restricted legal sense: the acquisition of a national passport and therefore the full range of rights that are available only to citizens. On this narrower question, there is much less scholarly work (Gordon 2007; Hansen and Weil 2002; Howard 2006: 443–455; IPSO REID/Dominion Institute 2007; Wilcox 2004). This policy brief will not attempt to provide a comprehensive account of the causes of recent changes in citizenship policy. Nor will it directly address overly abstract questions of what citizenship should look like according to theories of justice. Rather, it will look at how different citizenship policies produce different integration outcomes. The appropriate policy, therefore, depends directly on what policymakers want to achieve.

---

1   For instance, global citizenship, ecological citizenship, cultural citizenship, diasporic citizenship, local citizenship and sexual citizenship. On this, see Brubaker 2004.

99

In this policy brief, integration is understood in civic and socioeconomic rather than cultural terms. Integration, in our definition, has three pillars:

1. Eliminating the gap between an immigrant/ethnic minority population's economic and educational outcomes and those of the overall population.
2. Ensuring that all migrant groups respect a common legal framework.
3. Ensuring that the segregation of such groups in any particular sphere is voluntary rather than coerced.

When all three conditions are met, people are integrated. Understood this way, integration is consistent with both a high and a low degree of cultural difference. People may retain their cultural background, trade it in for that of the host country or (mostly commonly) create a synthesis of the two, as they wish.

The policy brief will proceed in three steps. First, it will provide a brief empirical overview of citizenship policy in major European and North American states. Second, it will summarize recent changes in citizenship policy for a key set of countries. Finally, it will provide policy-relevant conclusions on the likely effects of particular policy changes. (An annex on future research questions is also included.)

The policy brief argues that recent pan-European changes to citizenship policy—the introduction of ceremonies and citizenship and language tests—can make a small but observable difference in integration outcomes. However, only a broader set of integration policies will lead to improved socioeconomic outcomes among minority groups in Europe. These policies include measures designed to ensure that first-generation immigrants acquire the language at or after settlement, and education policies that ensure full language acquisition by the second generation.

Empirical Overview

There are two key elements to this empirical overview. The first is a comparison of citizenship acquisition in Europe and North America, namely what the principal elements are and how they differ. The second explores how rates of naturalization differ from country to country.

Citizenship Acquisition

Many authors distinguish between countries according to whether they have ethnic or political citizenship, whether it is *jus sanguinis* (citizenship by descent) or *jus soli* (citizenship by birth) (Brubaker 1992).

This is a false dichotomy. All liberal democratic states allow citizenship by descent, and most have at least some provisions for citizenship by residence (Howard 2006: 443–455). The relevant questions are not merely whether a country distinguishes by descent or by birth but are rather the following:

1. How do the descent and residence requirements operate? For those born in the country, do they secure citizenship automatically by being born in the territory or are there other criteria in addition to place of birth (pure vs. conditional *jus soli*)?
2. How many years of residence are required to acquire citizenship?
3. What other requirements are attached to the naturalization process (language, good conduct, etc.)?
4. Are individuals required to relinquish other nationalities or is dual citizenship tolerated?

These four questions result in very different answers for different countries.

Table 1: Citizenship policy in Europe, North America and Australia

	Australia	Britain	Canada	France	Germany	Netherlands	US
Years of residence[1]	4	6	3	5	8	5	5
Good conduct requirement[2]	Yes	Yes	Yes	Yes	Yes	Yes	Yes
Language requirement	Yes	Yes	Yes	Yes	Yes	Yes	Yes
Citizenship test	Yes	Yes	Yes	No	Yes	Yes	Yes
Values test	Yes	Yes	No	No	No	Yes	No
Dual citizenship[3]	Yes	Yes	Yes	Yes	No (with many exemptions)	No (with many exemptions)	Yes
Automatic right for the 2nd generation	Yes	Yes	Yes	Yes	Yes	Yes	Yes[4]

1 Across the European Union, residency requirements range from three years (Belgium) to ten years (Austria, Greece, Italy, Portugal and Spain) (Waldrauch n.d.: 37).

2 Such rules exist in all EU states, though they can be (as in Italy, Portugal and Spain) very vague (Waldrauch n.d.: 42).

3 Looking at other EU countries, Belgium, Finland, France, Greece, Ireland, Italy, Portugal and Sweden also tolerate dual citizenship. Austria, Denmark and Luxembourg do not (Waldrauch n.d.: 39).

4 Only Greece, Austria and Spain do not provide for an automatic right (declaration) to citizenship, relying on discretionary naturalization or the 'option' model. See Harald Waldrauch, 'Acquisition of Nationality.'

Naturalization Rates

The rate of naturalization is the second empirical element of note. The key point is that the major receiving countries have sharply varying naturalization rates, from a low rate in Germany to higher rates in the Netherlands and Sweden. Figure 1 lays out the naturalization rates for six of the key European countries.

Recent Changes in Citizenship Policies

Since 1989, citizenship policies—understood as the conditions under which individuals acquire national citizenship—have changed in Europe and in North America. Residency requirements (the number of years that people may live in a country before acquiring citizenship) have been decreased in some countries (Belgium, Germany) and increased in others (Greece, Spain, Italy, Britain); social rights have been

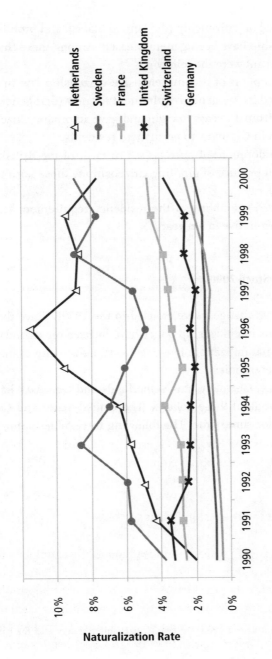

Figure 1. Naturalization rates, 1990 to 2000

Source: Waldrauch and Çinar 2003.

made conditional on citizenship (the United States); and prohibitions on dual citizenship have been generally eased. Among these changes, the most significant were the following:

- *Germany's* adoption of a comprehensive citizenship law in 2000, which reduced its residency requirement for new (first-generation) immigrants from 15 years to eight and gave automatic citizenship to those born in Germany to permanent residents.
- *Ireland's* abandonment of pure *jus soli* in favor of the British (and now German) practice of granting citizenship to those born to permanent residents.
- *Italy and Greece's* doubling of the residency requirement for new immigrants from five to ten years.

Policy Changes Since 2000

Most of the above changes were enacted in the 1990s. Since the millennium, reforms in citizenship policy have focused on secondary requirements for naturalization: language tests, citizenship exams and naturalization ceremonies.

Britain, France, Germany, the Netherlands and Denmark have all adopted some or all of these policies. The United States and Canada have had them for some time. The following three tables summarize these policies.[2]

---

2 Note that in a number of cases, the civics/citizenship test serves as the language test.

Table 2: Language tests in Europe, North America and Australia (2002 figures)

	Australia	Britain	Canada	France	Germany	Netherlands	US
For residence	Indirect	Yes	Indirect	Yes	Yes	Yes	No
For citizenship	Combined with civics test	Yes	Combined with civics test	Yes	Yes	Yes	Combined with civics test)
Level*	Modest	Inter-mediate	Modest	Related to one's profession	Inter-mediate (B1)	Modest (A2)	Inter-mediate
Costs[1]	AUD 280 (for naturalization)	GBP 34	Naturalization fee: CAD 200	Free	EUR 55 residence Naturalization fee EUR 255	EUR 350 + 65 for the DVD Naturaliza-tion fee: EUR 229–344 (depending on income)	Naturalization fee: USD 595

* Where rankings (B1) are included, they refer to the six proficiency levels specified by the Common European Framework of Reference. There are 3 broad levels (A–C, with A the lowest), with two sublevels in each (A1, A2, B1, B2, C1, C2). Level 1 is lower than Level 2. More information available online: www.coe.int/t/dg4/linguistic/cadre_EN.asp?

1 Naturalization fees very greatly across the EU, from nothing in France, Belgium, Italy and Spain to Euro 1,470 in Greece (Waldrauch n.d.: 33).

Table 3: Citizenship/civics tests in Europe, North America and Australia

	Australia	Britain	Canada	France	Germany	Netherlands	US
Test	Yes	Yes	Yes	No	Under discussion	Yes	Yes
Content	Responsibilities and privileges of citizenship, values, history, government	Migration to Britain, role of women/ family/ population/ regions, religion/ tolerance, customs/ traditions	Voting procedures, history and geography, rights and responsibilities of citizenship			Knowledge of Dutch society, history, politics, law, work, education and health care	Government and history. From October 2008 a new test will cover fundamental concepts of American democracy, basic US history and the rights and responsibilities of citizenship
Cost	AUD 280 (naturalization)	GBP 34 UK, naturalization fee GBP 655	CAD 200 (naturalization)			EUR 350	USD 400
Pass rate	92.9%	67.4%	90%			90%	84%

In some cases, new language requirements are supported by language classes. Table 4 summarizes language training in select European countries, North America and Australia.

The tables provide a cross-section of the various secondary requirements now necessary for naturalization across the transatlantic space. This policy brief now turns to in-depth case studies of several key countries, first in Europe then in North America.

It is important to note that although language and citizenship tests are new to Europe, they have a long history in the traditional settler countries of North America. Indeed, many of the requirements that are viewed as inherently anti-immigrant in Europe have long been maintained in Canada and the United States, as well as in Australia.

United Kingdom

The United Kingdom first introduced changes to citizenship policy in response to two events in 2001—Asian-White riots in northern England and the September 11 attacks—and British political scientist Bernard Crick's report on citizenship published in 2003. Following the London transit bombings of July 7, 2005, citizenship policy was further reformed.

Citizenship Ceremonies

Since 2004, naturalizing Britons have had to take part in a citizenship ceremony during which they swear allegiance to Queen Elizabeth II (as Head of State) and sing the national anthem. They also pledge to respect the United Kingdom's basic rights and freedoms and uphold its democratic values. The overall naturalization fee (GBP 655) covers the citizenship ceremony, including the salaries of officials and the lunch provided (in 2004, this component was GBP 68).

Table 4: Language training in Europe, North America and Australia

	UK	France	Germany	Netherlands	Australia	Canada	US
Hours	Varies	400 + 1 day civics	600–900 + 45 civics	600 (average)	400	Varies, but often 6 weeks	Varies; much occurs within schools
Who Pays	Candidate (state pays for refugees and long-standing residents)	State	Federal government	Participant (if successful, they recover 70% of costs)	State	State, provinces, cities	Federal government and states
Compulsory	No	Yes, if determined by interview	Yes (those resident in Germany can volunteer)	Yes	No	No	No
Funding				EUR 270 million		CAD 284 million	USD 1 billion

As of 2005, the citizenship ceremonies were supplemented with citizenship (or "civics") tests. They serve as a test of both language and citizenship; if applicants can take and pass the citizenship test, it is taken as evidence of their fluency in English (or Gaelic). Those who are not sufficiently fluent may instead take combined English for Speakers of other Languages (ESOL) and citizenship classes. If applicants are uncertain of their English-language level, they may go to a "learn direct center" (centers providing information on jobs) for assessment. After taking the test, applicants may apply for naturalization. In 2007, the test became a requirement both for those wishing to naturalize and those wanting to become permanent residents.

The test is made up of 24 computer-based questions. Applicants must answer 18 out of 24 questions correctly (a score of 75 percent). Applicants are given 45 minutes to complete the test (more if they have a medical condition) and they may take a practice test before beginning. Most of the questions are about the United Kingdom in general, but there are also questions specific to the applicant's place of residence. While the general areas cover some history, culture and demographics, the emphasis is on political knowledge, education and health. The cost of the test is GBP 34 with the fee likely to increase in the future.

France

Under President Jacques Chirac (1995 to 2007), the French government increased its emphasis on civic integration (which chiefly involves language) in addition to its interest in immigration reform. France has no citizenship ceremonies although current President Nicolas Sarkozy is in favor of them. There is an accelerated citizenship process for students who have graduated from a French university (a reduction of three years).

For residence: Migrants admitted to France for the first time and who wish to reside in the country must sign a "reception and integration" contract. Since 2003, all new migrants to France must take a one-day civics class and—unless they are native French speakers (estimated to be one-third of the some 150,000 migrants who arrive in France each year)—400 hours of French language instruction (Joppke 2007: 336–338). In addition, those wishing to obtain a ten-year residence permit (the chief means to citizenship for first-generation immigrants) need to fulfill three requirements:

1. Commit to abide by the principles and laws governing the French Republic.
2. Show compliance with such principles and laws (evinced by no criminal record).
3. Demonstrate a knowledge of French suitable for their professional position.

For citizenship: Those wishing to naturalize must pass a language test. Applicants are summoned to their local police station for an interview within a few months of applying for citizenship. The interview is meant to ensure that the applicant understands and speaks fluent French, abides by French laws and principles, and still resides in France (if the applicant is requesting citizenship by marriage, the interview at the local police station must also ensure that the couple lives in the same household). The language test takes the form of a conversation with a police officer, who asks information about where the applicant lives, what he/she does, and so on.

Upon becoming president in 2007, Sarkozy created a Ministry of Immigration, Integration, National Identity and Co-development. While thus far it has kept a low profile, further changes to citizenship policy may yet be forthcoming.

The Netherlands

The Netherlands turned away from a policy of multiculturalism and toward more proactive integration after a series of events from 2000 onward. The first was an essay published in 2000 that opened the door to public debates on the failures of multiculturalism. The second was the murder in 2002 of politician Pim Fortuyn—who believed the Netherlands should integrate immigrants before allowing new ones to settle—and the subsequent success of his party in parliamentary elections. The third was the murder in 2004 of filmmaker Theo van Gogh, whom a dual Dutch-Moroccan citizen killed for collaborating on a film critical of Islam.

The centerpiece of Dutch policy is the "civic integration exam" required for nationals of most countries outside the EU. All such nationals who want to be in the Netherlands for more than 90 days (for temporary or permanent residence or naturalization) must take the exam. Those naturalizing must also participate in a citizenship ceremony.

The Civic Integration Exam

The exam consists of two parts: knowledge of Dutch society and Dutch language skills. Knowledge of Dutch society is based on a film called *Coming to the Netherlands (Naar Nederland)*, which provides information about Dutch history, politics, law, work, education and health care. The film also contains scenes of women sunbathing nude on the beach and men kissing (though these have been edited out for countries where such images are illegal).

The language examination tests whether an applicant for a temporary residence permit (known as an MVV, which permits entry to a person planning to remain in the Netherlands for over three months) has attained a basic level of Dutch. The examination only tests speech and listening skills; there is no reading or writing requirement. Applicants must be able to repeat sentences, answer short questions, indicate opposites, and repeat two different short stories.

The test for those in the country is somewhat more demanding than the test for those from abroad. An applicant within the Netherlands must show that he/she "can understand sentences and frequently used expressions related to areas of most immediate relevance (e.g., very basic personal and family information, shopping, local geography, employment); can communicate in simple and routine tasks requiring a simple and direct exchange of information on familiar and routine matters; and can describe in simple terms aspects of his/her background or current environment and matters of urgency." (Common European Framework of Reference for Languages 2001: 24)

The candidate must cover the cost of the lessons and the exam (EUR 350; loans are available). Successful applicants can claim as much as 70 percent of the total cost back. Municipalities offer free courses for select groups such as refugees, spiritual advisors and specific groups of welfare recipients, including the elderly.

Naturalization

The integration exam officially replaced the naturalization test for non-EU citizens on January 1, 2007. Completion of the integration exam serves as a basic requirement for citizenship (Nana 2007).

Citizenship Ceremonies

Since October 2006, foreigners who pass the integration examination and fulfill naturalization requirements must take part in a naturalization ceremony. Officially, the test is meant to: (1) bestow a sense of pride on the part of those naturalizing, (2) give meaning to the naturalization process, (3) encourage applicants to think about the rights and duties of citizenship and (4) link the new citizen to his or her local government (where the ceremony takes place). Municipalities must hold at least one naturalization ceremony per year and applicants must go through the ceremony within a year of qualifying for citizenship.

Germany

German law distinguishes between naturalizations by right *(Anspruchs-einbürgerungen)* and naturalizations by discretion *(Ermessenseinbürger-ungen)* (Green 2001). Until 1990, all naturalizations were discretionary. Naturalization policy is implemented by the German federal states *(Länder)* (leading to the curious outcome that it is easier to become German in Berlin than in Bavaria), but was until 2000 guided by federal naturalization guidelines. From 1990, those born and schooled in Germany could naturalize by right (or enjoyed a right to naturalization); from 2000, those born of people who have lived in Germany for eight years and hold a permanent residency permit are German at birth (Green 2004).

In the case of discretionary naturalizations, a number of conditions apply. Germany has language and citizenship requirements for those wishing to naturalize, as well as a language test for spouses from particular countries. The country also offers integration courses for new immigrants.

Integration Courses

The Immigration Act of January 2005 requires that non-EU immigrants and ethnic Germans take a federally administered integration course consisting of basic and intermediate German, as well as an orientation course to familiarize participants with Germany history, culture and law. This involves up to 900 (originally 600) hours of language instruction plus 45 (originally 30) hours of civics training.

The language component is designed to provide participants with adequate proficiency, understood as the level that allows immigrants to deal with everyday situations on their own, to conduct conversations and to express themselves in writing commensurate with their age and education.

All new immigrants to Germany must attend the courses, but those resident in Germany may do so voluntarily. The cost for the courses is nominal—one Euro per hour of instruction—and is waived for individuals receiving social assistance (as first- and second-generation migrants do in disproportionate numbers).

The civics component is intended to give immigrants an understanding of the system of government and state administration in Germany, in particular the significance of free and democratic order, the party system, Germany's federalist structure, the welfare system, equal rights, tolerance and religious freedom.

Successful participants can demonstrate their proficiency in the language examination leading to the *Zertifikat Deutsch*, an official language certificate developed by the Goethe-Institute (B1 equivalent).

Finally, in 2007 the German government introduced a further language requirement: new spouses from countries for which visas are required to visit Germany (including Turkey) are required to pass a basic language test (amounting to several hundred words) *before* coming to Germany. The test is justified on the grounds that many spouses who do not work will not in practice take the integration courses, but the measure is also designed to discourage foreign brides.

Naturalization: Citizenship and Language Tests

On January 1, 2006, the German federal state of Baden-Württemberg instituted a citizenship test to be applied to applicants for naturalization from 57 Islamic countries (some 60 percent of all immigrants to Baden-Württemberg in 2004). The federal state of Hesse created a similar test. Other candidates for naturalization were subject to the procedure in exceptional cases ("New Rules for Muslims in German State Blasted" 2006).

The questions—which included topics such as attitudes towards wife beating, Israel and homosexuality—were widely viewed as targeting Muslims and provoked considerable controversy. In the Bundestag (Federal Parliament of Germany), the "Muslim tests" were met with widespread disdain from members of the Green Party, the Left

Party, the Social Democrats and the Free Democrats. There was also pressure for national standards. German integration commissioner Maria Böhmer said that "a person becomes a citizen of Germany, after all—not of a German state" (Corbett 2006).

On May 5, 2006, after months of political wrangling, the interior ministers of Germany's 16 federal states agreed on a set of common standards governing language and citizenship courses for migrants applying for a German passport. They agreed that all applicants in future will have to attend citizenship classes consisting of language and integration courses designed by the Federal Office for Migration and Refugees. The classes include learning about the basic values of the German constitution and state (Hawley 2006).

Canada

In Canada, immigrants can naturalize after three years of residence over four years—generous terms compared with other countries. Individuals may count time they spent in Canada before becoming permanent residents and, as long as the person's family is established in Canada, the individual may spend substantial time abroad during that three-year period.

Language Abilities

Immigrants are not tested directly for their language abilities before immigrating. That said, under the points system by which immigrants are admitted into Canada—for which there are currently proposals for reform before Parliament—applicants are given a maximum of 24 points (out of a required 67) for knowledge of both official languages (French and English), but 16 points for only one of them. Naturalization, by contrast, requires knowledge of one of the two official languages sufficient to be able "to communicate with people", that is, to be able to understand and to make oneself understood.

To help prepare citizenship applicants for the test, the federal government—in cooperation with provincial governments, school boards, community colleges and immigrant and community organizations—offers free language training across the country for adult permanent residents. In most provinces, the name of the program is "Language Instruction for Newcomers to Canada" (LINC) (Citizenship and Immigration Canada 2003). Provinces and (sometimes) cities also offer training courses, so in practice spending on language training is much higher than the LINC budget.

Citizenship Test

All naturalizing citizens under the age of 55 must demonstrate their language abilities and "knowledge of Canada" through a citizenship test (Citizenship and Immigration Canada 2007). It is usually a written test, but applicants can take oral tests in front of a citizenship judge if they cannot read or write English or French.

The exam is based on *A Look at Canada*, a free, government-issued booklet. Topics covered include rights and responsibilities of citizenship; social and cultural history (e.g., which three Aboriginal groups are recognized in the Constitution); Canadian politics; and both physical and political geography (e.g., how many provinces Canada has and the names of their capital cities).

Both the test and the applicant's interaction with the staff of Citizenship and Immigration Canada demonstrate language abilities. Applicants have to be able to understand simple spoken statements and questions, and they need to be able to communicate simple information.

Applicants who fail the test are asked to appear for a short interview (15 to 30 minutes) with a citizenship judge. At that interview, the judge asks them questions orally, giving them a second chance to meet the language and knowledge requirements.

Applicants who pass the citizenship test are invited to attend a citizenship ceremony that requires them to swear an oath of citizenship (Citizenship and Immigration Canada 2007). Citizenship ceremonies take place across the country and throughout the year, with special ceremonies on Canada Day (July 1) and during Citizenship Week (third week of October). Community groups are often involved in hosting the ceremonies. Applicants who successfully complete the process are given a citizenship certificate.

United States

American naturalization requirements are specified by the Immigration and Nationality Act (INA). They include the following:
- a period of continuous residence and physical presence in the United States;
- residence in a particular district prior to filing;
- an ability to read, write and speak English;
- a knowledge and understanding of US history and government;
- good moral character;
- an attachment to the principles of the US Constitution and form of government in the United States;
- an oath of allegiance to the United States.

All naturalization applicants must demonstrate good moral character, attachment and allegiance to the United States. The other naturalization requirements may be modified or waived for certain applicants, such as those serving in the military during a period of conflict which the president has specified with an executive order.

Applicants are eligible to naturalize if they have been lawful permanent residents in the country for at least five years prior to filing; for spouses of US citizens the requirement is three years. There can be no single absence from the United States of more than one year and absences of more than six months may disrupt the applicant's continuity of residence.

Generally, an applicant must show that he or she has been a person of good moral character for at least the statutory period prior to filing for naturalization. Good moral character is judged according to the absence of a criminal conviction for an "aggravated felony" (as defined by the Immigration and Nationality Act) or of involvement in other criminal activity.[3]

Language

Applicants for naturalization must be able to read, write, speak and understand words in ordinary usage in the English language. The requirement is waived for those over age 50 with 20 years residence in the United States. Although the language requirement is waived for this group, they must still take the civics portion of the naturalization exam. The federal government provides some funding for English as a Second Language (ESL) for adults but the need for high-value and high-quality English language and literacy instruction remains significant and unmet by the current system.[4] For example, the Migration Policy Institute estimates that it will take 277 million hours of English

---

3   See INA 101(a)(43) for the full definition of crimes that constitute "aggravated felonies". See also U.S. Citizenship and Immigration Services, General Naturalization Requirements.

4   Provision of high-quality adult English language instruction is inconsistent across the 50 states and has been criticized for "the unintegrated character of programs serving civics, workforce and family literacy needs; problems with teacher quality and professionalization; the system's lack of emphasis on distance or 'on-demand' learning; and low retention and persistence rates" (McHugh, Gelatt and Fix 2007: 13).

language instruction a year, for six years, to bring current adult Lawful Permanent Residents to a level of English proficiency needed to pass the naturalization test for adults age 25 and older or to begin postsecondary education for youth age 17 to 24 (McHugh, Gelatt and Fix 2007: 6).

Citizenship Test

Applicants demonstrate that they have met the US requirements for citizenship by taking a naturalization test, which was recently changed following a five-year review. The new test, to be implemented in full beginning October 2008, aims to be "standardized, fair and meaningful" (U.S. Citizenship and Immigration Services 2007). The revised test further emphasizes the fundamental concepts of American democracy, basic US history and the rights and responsibilities of citizenship. However, its general format—a list of 100 questions from which ten are asked of the applicants—is still the same. It remains to be seen how, if at all, the new test will affect naturalization patterns in the United States.

As in Canada, the civics portion of the naturalization test provides an additional opportunity for naturalization applicants to demonstrate English language ability. Applicants must converse with the naturalization interviewer and read and/or write a simple statement in English.

Citizenship Ceremony

If the United States Citizenship and Immigration Services (USCIS) approves an applicant for naturalization, a Notice of Naturalization Oath Ceremony (Form N-445) will be sent via mail to notify the applicant of the time and date of his or her Naturalization Oath Ceremony. In some places, applicants can choose to take the oath on the same day as their citizenship test (U.S. Citizenship and Immigration Services 2008).

Applicants who do not have the option of taking the oath on the same day as their interview must submit Form N-445 upon arriving at the Naturalization Oath Ceremony and must answer several questions on the form, including whether the applicant has traveled outside the United States since his or her interview with USCIS and whether he or she has claimed an exemption from military service. Applicants must also turn in their Permanent Resident Cards.

The main purpose of the citizenship ceremony is for an applicant to swear an oath of allegiance to the United States before a recognized official; this is the final requirement for naturalization. The text of the oath is as follows: "I hereby declare, on oath, that I absolutely and entirely renounce and abjure all allegiance and fidelity to any foreign prince, potentate, state or sovereignty, of whom or which I have heretofore been a subject or citizen; that I will support and defend the Constitution and laws of the United States of America against all enemies, foreign and domestic; that I will bear true faith and allegiance to the same; that I will bear arms on behalf of the United States when required by the law; that I will perform non-combatant service in the armed forces of the United States when required by the law; that I will perform work of national importance under civilian direction when required by the law; and that I take this obligation freely without any mental reservation or purpose of evasion; so help me God" (American Immigration Center 2004).

In certain instances, where the applicant establishes that he or she is opposed—on the basis of religious teaching or belief—to any type of service in armed forces, USCIS will permit these applicants to take a modified oath of allegiance. An applicant must also show that he or she is attached to the principles of the Constitution of the United States.

Upon completion of the oath, applicants receive their Certificate of Naturalization and may apply for a US passport at the ceremony.

Often the Naturalization Oath Ceremony includes non-essential, non-mandatory proceedings such as an address from the presiding official and the singing of the American national anthem.

The Effects of Policy Changes on Integration

As most citizenship requirements in Europe are new, it is difficult to measure their effect on integration. Nonetheless, there are some early indicators. Furthermore, North America's long experience with all three requirements—language tests, civics tests and citizenship ceremonies—may serve as a reliable proxy.

Language and Social Integration

Extensive research in North America has confirmed that in a service-based economy in which the majority of new jobs are created in non-industrial sectors, mastery of the national language is key to economic success. In the mid-1990s, research commissioned by Human Resources and Social Development Canada showed that immigrants fluent in French or English (the two national languages) earned CAD 7,900 per year more on arrival. Over time, this income gap persists and actually increases slightly. Ten years after landing, immigrants who arrived with proficiency in either official language earn, on average, CAD 8,500 per year more than those who did not (1995 figures) (Human Resources and Social Development Canada 1996).

At the start of the millennium, Germany's government-appointed independent commission on immigration and integration (known informally as the Süssmuth commission) emphasized the centrality of the German language in ensuring the labor market success of immigrants and permanent residents in Germany (Süssmuth 2001). A recent Urban Institute study on immigrants to the American state of Arkansas arrived at the same conclusion: poor language skills among many recent Latino immigrants have inhibited their economic integration. The only hope for their children is success through the educational system, which, in turn, requires fluency in English (Researcher: Education Key in Immigrant Success 2007). None of this should be particularly surprising. In almost all professional and managerial positions, excellence in the national language is essential.

Language Tests

The French, German and Dutch language tests have had a measurably positive impact on language acquisition. Even in the case of the least-demanding test—for family immigrants to Germany—immigrants must understand several hundred words of German, itself a first step. More importantly, 600 to 900 hours of language instruction amounts to ten to 15 months of intensive German assuming three hours of class time per day, the equivalent of an intensive course at Germany's Goethe Institute.

There is no consensus in the literature about the time required to learn a foreign language; the only consensus is that the more time spent, the better (Otega and Iberr-Shea 2005). Institutes with a long history of language training can, however, provide rough guides. The Goethe Institute recommends 400 to 600 hours of language instruction before taking the B1 German certification, which is evidence that one can cope with any daily situation in German.[5] Similarly, the Alliance Française estimates that it takes 400 to 480 hours of instruction to achieve an "intermediate" level of French, understood as the ability to cope with daily situations, follow complex French over a familiar topic and discuss one's areas of interest at length.[6]

In December 2006, the German Home Office hired a Danish consulting firm to report on the effects of the new integration courses. It concluded that the courses resulted in a "clear, qualitative improve-

5   More precisely, that those taking the exam "have a sufficient foundation in colloquial German to equip them to cope with all daily linguistic situations; that they have an extensive (wesentlichen) grasp of the grammatical structure and are able to lead and participate in conversations about daily life. They will also be able to express themselves in words or writing about simple events, as well as to read a texts on such events." From the Goethe Institute, www.goethe.de/ins/de/ler/kst/enindex.htm.

6   Specifically, to be able to "understand extended speech and follow complex lines of arguments provided the topic is reasonably familiar; interact with a degree of fluency and spontaneity that makes regular interaction with native speakers quite possible; present clear, detailed descriptions on a wide range of subjects related to my field of interest; and explain a viewpoint on a topical issue, giving the advantages and disadvantages of various options." From Alliance Francaise and Centre for French Teaching Documentation, www.frenchcentreenugu.org/programs.html#q2.

ment in German integration policy" (Evaluation der Integrationskurse nach dem Zuwanderungsgesetz 2006). Three-quarters of the participants took at least one official German-language test during their course (ibid.: 48). Of those that took a test after 300 hours, 69.8 percent secured the *Zertifikat Deutsch* (level B1) and 15.8 percent achieved one level higher (A1) (ibid.). On the downside, once those who did not take the test are factored in, it was clear that for 40 percent of all participants, 600 hours of German was not enough to reach the B1 level.

The tests can be administered before or after migrating. Administering them before departure gives migrants a greater incentive to study. For instance, since the German law was passed, prospective Turkish migrants have been scrambling to learn German (ibid.). Administering tests after arrival can, if they are taken seriously, lead to a better grasp of the national language as those preparing for them will have the opportunity to use it in everyday life. Naturally, this last advantage may not be achieved if immigrants move to predominantly foreign-language-speaking neighborhoods.

However, language courses can only do so much on their own. They only concern the first generation, many of whom will only ever require a functional level of Dutch or German (English and French present special cases because of their international status and widespread use in former colonies).

Similarly, these requirements do not apply to EU nationals. In most cases, however, EU nationals travel from one country to another for purposes of work (OECD 2007: 11), which means that they either know enough of the national language (such as Polish laborers in the United Kingdom) or are able to work in another language. However, only four percent of Europeans have ever lived outside their country of citizenship and annual cross-border mobility amounts to 0.2 percent of the working-age European population (OECD 2007: 11). This figure compares with 1.5 percent in Canada and 3.5 percent in the United States.

The crucial generation for immigrant integration is the second: it is imperative that states do more to ensure they learn the national language. To do so, policymakers need to keep an open mind with respect to radical alternatives (busing students to overcome neighborhood effects, ending or curtailing streaming) and study the best practices of countries such as Canada or Sweden, which manage high levels of immigration.

Civics/Citizenship Tests

Citizenship tests play a modest but measurable role in ensuring immigrant integration in that they create a more informed (new) citizenry. Content is crucial and can ensure that all naturalizing citizens have a basic knowledge of a country's institutions, history and (possibly) basic moral commitments. They are no different than school (or driving) tests in that respect. In developing such tests, a number of points should be borne in mind:

- Content: Test-takers are more likely to view tests on history and institutions as important, and such tests are more likely to gain consensus support in the broader society. Tests on geography (e.g., major mountain ranges), popular culture (e.g., rock stars) or values (e.g., attitudes on public nudity) are less so, and the last case may well be inconsistent with liberal democratic values. For example, opposing homosexuality, as long as it is distinct from discriminating against homosexuals, is not inconsistent with citizenship per se.
- Form: Tests can be single answer, multiple-choice or long answer. Canada recently moved from single/short answers to multiple-choice tests. These have the advantage of being cheaper to administer and mark, but the migrants themselves view them as too easy and formalistic. In a similar vein, questions that ask for short, reflective answers ("Why is freedom of the press important?") will lead to more considered and genuine responses. There is a trade-off here: these questions produce more considered responses, but may be more difficult for immigrants with poorer language skills and less education.

In any policy area, implementation is as important as the formal policy itself. Literacy tests in particular have a dark history: they were used throughout the southern United States to disenfranchise African Americans. In a similar way, language and citizenship could be made exceptionally difficult with the specific aim of deterring and blocking applications for citizenship. This is effectively what Latvia did when it linked social rights and language acquisition with the specific aim of excluding the country's large Russian-speaking population (McNamara and Shohamy 2008).

Understood strictly in terms of the level of language required, the tests cannot be viewed as barriers. The cases studied here demand a minimum level of linguistic competence and in many cases are sensitive to the person's role in society. This is not, however, the only issue. Another central factor is whether or not the language test is linked with language training, as is the case in France, Germany, Britain and the Netherlands (though not for family reunification in the last case).

Referring to the Netherlands, sociologist Christian Joppke concluded in a 2007 journal article that since "no Dutch education programs exist abroad[,] integration from abroad boils down to no integration at all." (Joppke 2007: 335) This is overstating the case—the burden of integration is shifted from the state to the applicant—but the requirement clearly raises significant hurdles that prospective immigrants must overcome. This is deliberate: The government wishes to ensure that those who do arrive speak at least rudimentary Dutch; better still, foreigners resident in the Netherlands may look for spouses down the street rather than outside the country.

These are not the only potential barriers. Others include costs and scheduling. In some cases, such as the Netherlands and the US, the costs are high (particularly so for those taking the test abroad). High costs will inevitably discourage applicants with fewer resources. Whether this barrier is unreasonable depends on one's point of view and on the type of immigration scheme about which one is speaking. If family immigration is viewed as a right, then the cost in these countries for family immigration seems unreasonably high. For others, the "prize" on offer—residence and eventually citizenship—is immense.

For those undertaking language training within the country, the scheduling of the classes can be as important as the costs. If they interfere with work and/or childcare duties, then taking them may be practically impossible or pose undue strains on family life.

A further danger is that the policies will be framed as punitive and blocking when right-wing (and even far-right) parties support them and when the immigrant organizations define them as such. It is very important to emphasize that these requirements accompany a post-1990s openness to immigration in the major European receiving countries. This is not a subjective judgment. For the first time in 25 years, it is possible to immigrate—without family connections and outside the asylum system—to Britain, France and Germany.

It is, to be sure, one thing to open the doors to immigrants and another to ensure that a country is attractive to them. In addition to opposing xenophobia (which all European governments do), official rhetoric should emphasize that immigrants are welcome as full members of society. Rhetoric costs little, but can produce positive results. In this context, it is noteworthy that although Germany has, for the first time in decades, the legislative framework for accommodating immigration, it receives in practice very few immigrants.

Citizenship Ceremonies

The effect of citizenship ceremonies on integration is small but positive. Clearly they can have little impact on language acquisition or long-term labor market outcomes. When properly conducted (meaning that those involved take them seriously and governments conduct them in attractive surroundings), they can imbue the citizenship process with more meaning than is gained from a purely bureaucratic process. Local studies of citizenship ceremonies in Britain showed that those taking part appreciated them and felt that they added to the experience (Rimmer 2007: 7–8). More broadly, comparative research sponsored by the Home Office showed that citizenship ceremonies are valued by both the immigrants and the local politicians involved, and that the ceremonies "promote the value of naturalization." (Home Office 2001: 34)

The value of citizenship ceremonies depends on active participation in them. Their value, therefore, can be multiplied when more actors are involved. For example, a ceremony held in a school or community center can involve non-immigrants, especially when members of the local community are encouraged to serve as volunteers. Mock citizenship ceremonies in schools, with no naturalizing citizens involved, would have the added value of increasing an understanding of their content and importance among the broader public.

In all cases, the way in which citizenship ceremonies are conducted is very important. Done badly, they can be cold and impersonal. Done well, they can be (mildly) transformative for naturalizing citizens and buy much goodwill for little cost in the broader community.

Conclusions and Policy Recommendations

The available evidence from Europe and North America leads to two broad conclusions. First, intensive language training at the start of an immigrant's stay in his new country can produce highly positive results for integration. Second, making civics tests, language tests and citizenship ceremonies part of the naturalization process can have modest but positive effects on integration. However, as naturalization should ideally follow as well as contribute to integration, it is simply too late in the process to substantially affect labor market outcomes. From these points a number of recommendations follow:

1. Where immigration streams contain a large number of unskilled migrants, language requirements should be made a condition of settlement as well as of naturalization.
2. Funding should be provided for language courses and governments should make an effort to offer them on weekends and in the evenings and/or to provide daycare facilities. If the government wishes to have the migrants contribute, this should be in the form of loans.

127

3. Classes should be compulsory and there should be fines or other penalties for non-attendance. Carrots (such as Germany's offer of lower residency requirements for citizenship) as well as sticks should be used.
4. Family immigration raises difficult issues. It should be recognized as a right in the case of marriages that ensued before the immigrant moved to Europe. There is a distinction, in other words, between family immigration and family formation. As long as the ultimate right of family reunification is respected, the state may legitimately use policy to discourage foreign spouses.
5. Citizenship ceremonies should be maintained and a greater effort made to include as many members of the community as possible.
6. Mock and perhaps real ceremonies should be held in schools so as to introduce students to them and to their importance.
7. Civics tests are a reasonable and important requirement for acquiring a national passport and its advantages. They should focus on history and institutions rather than values.
8. It is perfectly legitimate for a state to shape values (as it does in the case of racism, discrimination, understandings of national history and so on), but the naturalization test is not the appropriate forum. The work should be done in the schools and in national or regional advertising campaigns.

All these requirements should be emphasized as basic and fair given the prize (access to a rich state's society, economy and citizenship), but they should be implemented with the goal of helping rather than penalizing immigrants, of providing them pathways rather than barriers and of emphasizing rather than downplaying the contribution they make to their new societies. The objective is integration, not exclusion.

The author is extremely grateful to Simon Green for sending me published and unpublished papers on the topic and for agreeing to be interviewed. For research assistance, I am grateful to Cliff Vanderlinden, Marieeve Reny, Jagtaran Singh, and Farzin Yousefian. For comments on this paper, I am grateful to Kirin Kalia, Will Somerville, Demetrios Papademetriou, Gregory A. Maniatis, and Michelle Mittelstadt, all of the Migration Polcy Institute; as well as to Rainer Bauböck and the other participants at the meeting of the Transatlantic Council for Migration in Bellagio, April 2008.

Annex: Future Research

The priorities for future research are clear. Particularly in Europe, citizenship ceremonies and language and citizenship tests are relatively new. It is important to explore in greater depth their role.

This has three components. First, public opinion research can now test the effect of the new requirements on the first cohort of test-takers as well as on the population as a whole. How positive was the experience? How much did they learn? Are they better able to cope in their new homes? Do they feel more British, German, French or Dutch following the citizenship ceremony? Does the existence of the tests have positive knock-on effects for broader public attitudes toward immigrants and minorities?

Second, studies can be done in both North America and Europe of these students' experiences in the classes themselves. In particular, where there is adequate data, students' results on entrance, at midterm and in the final tests will provide a simple and clear quantitative measure of their progress.

Finally, over the medium term, research can explore the impact of these requirements on immigrant integration and the social trajectories of the migrants who fulfilled them. Do those who took the test secure better jobs or educational certificates? Is there any measurable effect on ethnic minority performance overall? Is the language instruction offered, above all at the outset, sufficient to encourage better integration outcomes?

Further Reading

American Immigration Centre. Oath of Allegiance to the United States of America. 2004. www.us-immigration.com/information/citizenship_tutorial/oath.html (accessed May 23, 2008).

Bosniak, Linda. *The Citizens and the Alien: Dilemmas of Contemporary Membership*. Princeton, N.J.: Princeton University Press, 2006.

Brubaker, Rogers. *Citizenship and Nationhood in France and Germany.* Cambridge, Mass.: Harvard University Press, 1992.

Rogers Brubaker. In the Name of the Nation: Reflections on Nationalism and Patriotism. *Citizenship Studies* (8) 2: 115–127, 2004.

Carens, Joseph H. *Culture, Citizenship, and Community: A Contextual . Exploration of Justice as Even-handedness.* Oxford: Oxford University Press, 2000.

Citizenship and Immigration Canada. Welcome to Canada: What You Should Know: Language Training. 2003. www.cic.gc.ca/english/resources/publications/welcome/wel-22e.asp.

Citizenship and Immigration Canada. The citizenship test. 2007. www.cic.gc.ca/english/citizenship/cit-test.asp.

Common European Framework of Reference for Languages. Council of Europe. March 19, 2001. www.coe.int/t/dg4/linguistic/Source/Framework_EN.pdf (accessed March 21, 2008).

Corbett, Deanne. Testing the Limits of Tolerance. *Deutsche Welle.* March 16, 2006. www.dw-world.de/dw/article/0,2144,1935900,00.html.

Dutch Immigration and Naturalization Service (IND). Hoe kunt u Nederlander worden? www.ind.nl/en/Images/Ned_worden_0706_tcm6-574.pdf.

Dutch Immigration and Naturalization Service (IND). "Naar Nederland." www.naarnederland.nl/documentenservice/pagina.asp?pagkey=53768.

Evaluation der Integrationskurse nach dem Zuwanderungsgesetz. In *Abschlussbericht und Gutachten über Verbesserungspotenziale bei der Umsetzung der Integrationskurse.* Berlin: Bundesministerium des Innern, 2006.

Federal Ministry of the Interior. Integration of foreigners living in Germany. www.bmi.bund.de/cln_028/nn_122730/Internet/Content/Themen/Auslaender__Fluechtlinge__Asyl__Zuwanderung/Integration/Integration__der__bei__uns__lebenden__Auslaender__englisch.html.

Gordon, Susan M. Integrating Immigrants: Morality and Loyalty in US Naturalization Practice. *Citizenship Studies* (11) 4: 367–382, 2007.

Green, Simon. Citizenship Policy in Germany: The Case of Ethnicity over Residence. In *Towards a European Nationality*, edited by Randall Hansen and Patrick Weil. Houndmills: Palgrave, 2001: 24–51.

Green, Simon. *The Politics of Exclusion: Institutions and Immigration Policy in Contemporary Germany*. Manchester: Manchester University Press, 2004.

Hansen, Randall, and Patrick Weil. *Towards a European Nationality*. Houndmills: Macmillan, 2001.

Hansen, Randall, and Patrick Weil. *Dual Citizenship, Social Rights and Federal Citizenship in the US and Europe*. Oxford: Berghahn, 2002.

Hawley, Charles. The Search for Identity Continues. *Spiegel Online* May 9, 2006. www.spiegel.de/international/0,1518,415207,00.html.

Home Office. *Secure Borders, Safe Haven: Integration with Diversity in Modern Britain*. London: HMSO, 2001.

How Do I Become German? Ministers Have the Answer. *Deutsche Welle* May 5, 2006. www.dw-world.de/dw/article/0,2144,1994157,00.html.

Howard, Marc Morjé. Comparative Citizenship: An Agenda for Cross-National Research. *Perspectives on Politics* (4) 3: 443–455, 706, 2006.

Human Resources and Social Development Canada. The Importance of Language to Immigrants' Labour Market Outcomes. *Applied Research Bulletin* (2) 1 1995–1996. www.hrsdc.gc.ca/en/cs/sp/sdc/pkrf/publications/bulletins/1996-000005/page04.shtml.

IPSO REID/Dominion Institute. *The National Citizenship Exam 10-year Benchmark Study*. Toronto: Dominion Institute, 2007.

Joppke, Christian. Immigrants and Civic Integration in Western Europe. In *The Art of the State III: Belonging, Diversity, Recognition and Shared Citizenship in Canada*, edited by. Keith Banting, Thomas J. Courchene and F. Leslie Seidle. Montreal: Institute for Research in Public Policy, 2007: 321–350.

Kymlicka, Will. *Politics in the Vernacular: Nationalism, Multiculturalism, and Citizenship*. Oxford: Oxford University Press, 2001.

McHugh, Marige, Julia Gelatt and Michael Fix. *Adult English Language Instruction in the United States: Determining Need and Investing Wisely.* Washington, DC: Migration Policy Institute, 2007. www.migrationpolicy.org/pubs/NCIIP_English_Instruction 073107.pdf.

McNamara, Tim, and Elana Shohamy. Viewpoint: Language Tests and Human Rights. *International Journal of Applied Linguistics* (18) 1: 89–95, 2008.

Nana, Chavi Keeney. With Strict Policies in Place, Dutch Discourse on Integration Becomes More Inclusive. Migration Information Source. April 2007. www.migrationinformation.org/USfocus/display.cfm?id=596.

Naturalization Oath Ceremony. www.immihelp.com/citizenship/naturalization-oath-ceremony.html (accessed May 22, 2008).

New Rules for Muslims in German State Blasted. *Deutsche Welle.* January 5, 2006. www.dw-world.de/dw/article/0,2144,1840793,00.html.

OECD. Economic Survey of the European Union 2007. www.oecd.org/dataoecd/60/48/39311348.pdf.

OECD. Removing obstacles to geographic labour mobility. In *Economic survey of the European Union 2007.* Paris: OECD, 2007. www.oecd.org/document/61/0,3343,fr_2649_34111_39001853_1_1_1_1,00.html.

Ortega, Lourdes, and Gina Iberr-Shea. Longitudinal Research in Second Language Acquisition: Recent Trends and Future Directions. *Annual Review of Applied Lingusitics* (25) 2005: 26–45.

Researcher: Education Key in Immigrant Success. *The Morning News,* April 3, 2007. www.urban.org/UploadedPDF/411441_Arkansas_complete.pdf.

Rimmer, Mark. The Future of Citizenship Ceremonies, background paper for Lord Goldsmith's report on citizenship: Our Command Bond. 2007. www.justice.gov.uk/docs/goldsmith.pdf.

Süssmuth, Rita (ed.). *Zuwanderung gestalten — Integration fördern.* Berlin: Bundesministerium des Innern, 2001.

U.S. Citizenship and Immigration Services. General Naturalization Requirements. 2008. www.uscis.gov/portal/site/uscis/menuitem.

5af9bb95919f35e66f614176543f6d1a/vgnextoid=12e596981298d01
0VgnVCM10000048f3d6a1RCRD&vgnextchannel=96719c7755cb9
010VgnVCM10000045f3d6a1RCRD.

U.S. Citizenship and Immigration Services. Fact Sheet: USCIS Naturalization Test Redesign. Washington, DC: U.S. Department of Homeland Security, 2007. www.uscis.gov/files/pressrelease/Fact-SheetNatzTest113006.pdf.

U.S. Citizenship and Immigration Services. Frequently Asked Questions About Naturalization. 2008. www.uscis.gov/portal/site/uscis/menuitem.5af9bb95919f35e66f614176543f6d1a/vgnextoid=ee14b4ac0933e010VgnVCM1000000ecd190aRCRD&vgnextchannel=fe529c7755cb9010VgnVCM10000045f3d6a1RCRD.

Waldrauch, Harald. Acquisition of Nationality. In The International Migration, Social Cohesion and Integration (IMISCOE). Research project on "Acquisition and Loss of Nationality" (Principal Investigator: Rainer Bauböck) n.d. www.imiscoe.org/natac/documents/chapter_3_acquisition_of_nationality.pdf.

Waldrauch, Harald, and Dilek Çinar. Staatsbürgerschaftspolitik und Einbürgerungspraxis in Österreich. In *Österreichischer Migrations- und Integrationsbericht*, edited by Irene Stacher and Heinz Fassmann. Klagenfurt: Drava, 2003: 261–283.

Wilcox, Shelley. Culture, National Identity, and Admission to Citizenship. *Social Theory and Practice* (30) 2004: 559–582.

The Complexities of Immigration: Why Western Countries Struggle with Immigration Politics and Policies

Jennifer L. Hochschild, John Mollenkopf

Almost 200 million individuals, about three percent of the world's population, live outside the country where they were born, according to United Nations estimates. Over 100 million migrants live in the more developed regions of the world, including nine million in Northern Europe, 22 million in Western Europe and 38 million in the United States. Proportionally, nine percent of residents in Northern Europe, 12 percent in Western Europe and 13 percent in the United States are immigrants.[1] If we were to include their children born in these destinations (the so-called second generation), the figures would roughly double. The global number of migrants more than doubled between 1970 and 2002, and the number continues to rise.[2] As international migration flows expand, so do both the benefits and complexities for governments.

The political puzzles that high levels of immigration create may be even more difficult to solve than the economic, cultural or security puzzles. At any rate, they must take priority, since governments cannot promulgate and implement economic, cultural and security policies unless sufficient political forces are mustered. Immigrants should also make politics a priority (although they usually do not do

---

1   United Nations. International Migration 2006. The overall figure includes refugees displaced by conflict as well as the economic migrants who live in the more developed regions. www.un.org/esa/population/publications/2006Migration_Chart/2006 IttMig_chart.htm.

2   United Nations. International Migration Report 2002. www.un.org/esa/population/publications/ittmig2002/2002ITTMIGTEXT22-11.pdf

135

so). After all, immigrants will be successfully incorporated into their host countries only after they have enough involvement and influence in decision-making that they can help shape relevant policies. So politics matters—but for reasons we explain below, supporters of various ideologies in widely different countries all run into trouble when they consider immigration and immigrants.

Western liberal democracies enthusiastically promote free or only slightly restricted movement of information, capital, and goods and services—but not of people. Membership is simply too important for any government to relinquish control over who leaves and enters its territory. Clearly, control is never perfect, the composition of a country's population is never ideal and any sort of immigrant population will bring both benefits and costs. But every competent and rational state will seek to control its borders, attain the right balance of residents' skills and loyalties, and maximize the benefits of immigration while minimizing its costs.

There are no recipes here. Each state makes different choices to attain these goals and new leadership or changes in circumstances lead many states to change their choices over time. The policy issues are numerous, and are further complicated by the fact that immigrants from different nations present distinct demands, needs and values. Issues for policymakers include, but are not limited to:

- regularizing the status and future of undocumented immigrants;
- redesigning electoral systems and party structures to give immigrants a genuine political voice;
- developing and coordinating supranational policies toward immigrants and immigration;
- controlling hostility towards and violence against immigrants on the part of native-born residents, and vice versa;
- enabling churches and mosques, advocacy groups and civic organizations to integrate immigrants into communities;
- figuring out the implications of transnational sentiments and legal statuses;
- incorporating immigrants and their children into schools, jobs and neighborhoods;

136

- striving to prevent alienation and radicalization among poor, isolated, or ideologically motivated youth.

This policy brief does not address such issues despite their urgency and importance. Instead, we wish to explore the general political conundrums underlying them. Both the left and the right face normative and partisan differences over these policy choices within their own groups—as do immigrants themselves. Nevertheless, liberal democratic countries will need to somehow manage ideological and political disputes so they can address urgent cultural, economic, political and moral questions over the next few decades.

The Puzzle of Rising Immigration in Democratic Polities

To begin with, the very fact of immigration creates a central puzzle for democratic theory: for several decades, most Western countries have had high and rising levels of immigration even though a majority of their populations consistently want immigration to stabilize or decrease. This public sentiment has been apparent since the early 1960s, when survey researchers first began to investigate the question of immigration. Table 1 shows the pattern for 2003, the most recent year for which we have comparable data in North America and Europe:

Table 1: Views on desirable trajectories for immigration in selected Western nations, 2003

Country	Foreign-born population share in 2003 (percent)	Increase levels of immigration "a lot" + "a little" (percent)	Keep levels of immigration the same (percent)	Reduce levels of immigration "a little" + "a lot" (percent)
Austria	11.4	7	30	63
Canada	18.7	30	39	31
Denmark	6.3	10	39	50
France	7.8	8	27	66
Germany	12.9	4	23	73
Great Britain	8.9	6	16	78
Netherlands	10.7	4	27	70
Norway	7.6	8	22	70
Spain	5.3 (2001)	10	37	54
Sweden	12	12	31	57
Switzerland	23.1	6	50	44
United States	12.6	11	32	56

Note: For some countries, these results include non-citizen respondents, so the table probably overestimates voters' support for more immigration.
Sources: column 2: Organization for Economic Cooperation and Development (OECD), Table A.1.4 "Stocks of Foreign Born Population in Selected OECD Countries". www.publications.parliament.uk/pa/ld200708/ldselect/ldeconaf/82/8217.htm; columns 3–5: International Social Survey Program (ISSP), 2003.

With the notable exception of Canada, barely a tenth of the population of any of these countries favors increased immigration; half or more of the residents of these countries, except for Canada and Switzerland, want a decrease.

Governments pursue the opposite of what most voters want over a long period of time on a few other policies as well; the best example is free trade. But such policies are unusual, volatile and always subject to political challenge and the possibility of a populist revolt. Therefore, governments tend to react defensively about immigration. They are vulnerable to nativist pressures and make a big show of hostility toward illegal immigration—but they continue admitting large numbers of immigrants while turning a relatively blind eye to the undocumented. Immigrants are simply too important to the economy, demographic health and thus the fiscal health of host countries to be excluded, even if governments could keep them out. However, immigration policy and policies toward immigrants rest on a shaky foundation from the perspective of any political party seeking to win elections, and this political weakness has consequences for all immigration-related policies.

Ideological Conundrums

Problems for the Left

Within the context of popular distaste for immigration, native-born leftists in most Western nations are more welcoming to, or at least tolerant of, immigrants than are native-born rightists. Table 2 shows that members of left parties are consistently, if modestly, more favorable in their immigration position.

Table 2: Approval of immigration among supporters of the two largest political parties in selected Western nations, 2003

Country	Support for increasing immigration or keeping it at the same level			
	Largest party on the left (percent)		Largest party on the right (percent)	
Austria	SPOE	35	OEVP	31
Canada	Liberal	72	Conservative	62
Denmark	Social Democratic	56	Liberal	49
France	Socialist	49	UMP-Conservative	21
Germany	Social Democratic (SPD)	33	Christian Democratic/ Christ. Social (CDU/CSU)	22
United Kingdom	Labor	26	Conservative	14
Netherlands	Labor (PvdA)	39	Christian Democratic(CDA)	22
Norway	Labor	29	Progress	5
Spain	Socialist (PSOE)	50	Popular (PP)	39
Sweden	S (Social Democrats)	43	M (Liberal Conservative)	26
Switzerland	Social Democratic	73	Swiss Peoples	25
United States	Democratic	49	Republican	34

Note: The figures include respondents who favored increasing immigration "a lot" or "a little" or "keeping it at the same level". A large majority in both columns chose "the same". For some countries, the sample size for respondents identifying with even the two largest parties is small, so these figures are not completely reliable. Party labels were provided by ISSP.
Source: International Social Survey Program (ISSP), 2003.

These figures accord with our general understanding of left and right ideologies. Social democratic (in the European context) and liberal (in the American context) activists tend to be relatively more oriented toward the international arena and less isolationist.[3] They tend to be

3 The present American political configurations with regard to Iraq, and earlier with regard to Vietnam, are historical anomalies.

more culturally flexible or cosmopolitan in their commitments, if not necessarily in their behaviors, and they sympathize with the desire to escape poverty and oppression that drives many to emigrate from their home country. In recent years, European (and increasingly American) leftist support for Palestinians in the Middle East has augmented sympathy for Muslim immigrants.

Leftists also believe in respecting cultural differences and honoring group identities, often through explicit public policies of multiculturalism. But they disagree profoundly with many immigrants' gender practices, their treatment of children (particularly daughters) and their views on homosexuality. Especially but not only in Europe, leftists are insistently secular, so they may be uneasy about immigrants' religious commitments and practices. Leftist political actors may also worry that low-skilled immigrants will take jobs away from low-skilled, native-born workers. This dilemma is especially acute when the threatened native workers are disproportionately ethnic minorities, such as black descendents of slaves in the United States. So the left endorses at least some aspects of immigration but has many concerns about actual immigrants.

Problems for the Right

Political actors on the right also face ideological and partisan dilemmas. Rightists tend to be unenthusiastic about immigration per se, for reasons that are the mirror image of the left: they are more isolationist, more culturally and politically nationalist, more concerned about the rule of law and legal status per se and more inclined to rely on international markets than on migration to alleviate worldwide poverty. But rightists' views on gender and parental roles, homosexuality and religiosity accord much more with the views of many immigrants than they do with those of the leftists. Social conservatives are also more sympathetic to some immigrants' desire to bring religious values and practices into the public realm. Rightists, then, resist immigration but have much in common with a high proportion of actual immigrants.

The right faces additional dilemmas with regard to the political incorporation of immigrants. Although conservatives have little tolerance for illegal immigration, they sometimes manage or own businesses that depend on undocumented immigrant labor and the willingness of the immigrants to accept low wages and difficult working conditions. Industries of this sort, like a restaurant owners' association or a construction trades' association, can often be a potent national interest group. Conservatives might prefer regularizing the status of undocumented immigrants in order to maintain a stable workforce and to discourage the casual and widespread acceptance of illegality. Regularization would also eliminate the hypocrisy of the government spending tax revenues on border protection while employers hire workers who foil that protection—and generate profits that can be taxed. But conservatives find it unpalatable to publicly endorse "amnesty" in the United States or to be equivalently "soft" on undocumented immigrants in Europe.

The right faces an even deeper predicament regarding the ultimate goal of immigration policies and policies toward immigrants. Conservatives tend to be "national particularists" (in the words of political scientist Christian Joppke), meaning that they endorse unilateral assimilationism or liberal neutrality among individuals. But some conservatives are also nativists—and demonstrating hostility toward immigrants is not a good strategy for persuading them to assimilate. It is not easy for a political party or organization seeking to unify rightists to reconcile these two contradictory impulses.

Immigrants' Choices

Immigrants also get caught up in these conundrums, which surely affect them more deeply. Should immigrants ally with conservatives, who may hold similar cultural values and provide employment, but who may also oppose further immigration, want to exact a stiff price for incorporation and flirt with xenophobia? Or should they ally with leftists, who oppose and even scorn some of their cultural or religious values, but who might help enact their cultural preferences, provide more social services or support their access to the labor market?

The right strategy for building coalitions with other immigrants is just as unclear. Should immigrant groups ally with refugees, undocumented workers or highly skilled temporary workers, even if they come from a different part of the world and are otherwise dissimilar? Or should they seek to form coalitions with native-born residents of the same nationality or even of the same broad social class, in the hopes of avoiding competition over jobs and tension over status and resources? Another question: should immigrants aim to enter their new polity as individuals or as members of an ethnic group? Can they retain ties to their countries of origin while becoming a citizen of the receiving country; should they ally with co-religionists across national borders; should they permit or encourage their children to become full-fledged Germans, Dutch or Americans?

Variants of these questions have always faced migrants, as a rich literature of memoirs and histories shows. But some issues and options are new or have attained a new urgency in this era of easy international travel, of stateless organizations willing to use violence to attain their goals and of host countries increasingly nervous about security and national unity. For instance, Muslim immigrants might ponder how they can stay committed Muslims without being drawn into international radicalism, while migrants from former colonies might wonder how they can take advantage of their linguistic and cultural ties while avoiding demeaning ethnic stereotypes. And even the old questions have no settled answers.

Policy Choices

Cross-cutting political and ideological commitments not only make life complicated for party leaders, they also make it even more difficult for host countries to address political, cultural and economic questions. Like the partisan dilemmas, these policy dilemmas contribute to high levels of uncertainty about the eventual success of immigrant integration.

Economic Policies

Western nations face low birth rates and the retirement of native-born workers born during the baby boom. The native-born population also will not take certain jobs (especially dirty jobs) unless these jobs pay relatively well. This means Western nations must balance their need for immigrant workers to compensate for these circumstances with the need to regulate migrant flows, reduce unemployment and control public dependency. They appear unable to get this balance right for very long.

Nations have experimented with a variety of policies, for example: short- and long-term guestworker programs; higher and lower overall quotas; ignoring and cracking down on low-skilled undocumented immigrants; raising and lowering the number of slots for high-skilled immigrants; enhancing and limiting public services; expanding and contracting educational and language programs; encouraging workers to move to underdeveloped parts of the nation and concentrating them in major cities.

No single set of choices may be "right" over the long term for maintaining the balance between too many and too few workers of a given skill level. At best, a nation can hope to adopt intelligent policies that solve actual problems in the short term rather than pursuing partisan or ideological ends that have little to do with genuine economic needs or market forces. With luck and skill, together with appropriate advocacy and care, such policies need not sacrifice immigrants themselves for the sake of actual or perceived national imperatives.

Cultural Policies

Western nations must also balance the need for national integrity and unity with the appeal of diversity, of acquiring fresh ideas and energy, and of individuals and groups having the freedom to restyle their lives. Here, too, they may not be able to find the right balance or maintain any balance for long. Host countries have tried an array of policies: liberal neutrality, multiculturalism, national particularism, republican universalism, affirmative action, energetic assimilationist efforts, regional or national homogeneity, separatism, pillarization, transnationalism, supranational legislation and regulation, etc.

All of these policies have virtues and flaws, as well as exceptionally passionate advocates. Moreover, analysts and political activists disagree on what the virtues may be or whether overcoming the flaws requires a more intensive application of the same policies or shift to different ones. A nation should not expect stable solutions; rather it should aim for intelligent strategies that solve actual problems in the short run. This seems obvious, but is sometimes rare; politicians and advocates often find themselves promoting polarization in cultural arenas instead of adopting pragmatic, political compromises in cultural disputes.

Political Incorporation

Finally, political systems must strike a balance between too much and not enough openness towards new constituents, demands and activists. Political parties are always attuned to the forthcoming election and always compelled to respond to their current electoral base. But in order to thrive, they must also look to the future and appeal to new interests. This conundrum explains why the American Republican party (and the Democratic party to a lesser degree) is split between wanting to restrict immigration and punish illegal immigrants on the one hand and seeking to attract the huge pool of current and future Latino voters on the other.

Policymakers face a slightly different dilemma from political parties. Elected and appointed officials need stability and predictability in order to make and implement policies, but they must also accommodate major demographic shifts that inevitably change their tasks, especially in gateway cities and rapidly transforming small towns. That conundrum plays out in the institutions that have the least control over their circumstances and are closest to the most vulnerable among the native-born and immigrants: schools, religious organizations, social-service agencies, health-care providers and criminal justice systems. Policymaking may lose coherence under these cross-pressures. For example, in the United States some local jurisdictions have adopted harsh regulations against undocumented immigrants while others are working strenuously to cope with the presence of immigrants in ways that will benefit all residents (e.g., through programs of bilingual and adult education or new training for police and social-service workers).

Central-government officials must also balance domestic needs and pressures with those of the international or intergovernmental arena. Transnational links among countries, or the relationship between national and EU-level parliaments, will inevitably involve complex and simultaneous political negotiations. Once again, the search for ideal or even stable solutions may well be a waste of effort. The more appropriate goal is to try to steer the polity toward accommodating new groups without excessively disrupting the old ones.

Conclusion

Immigration has helped drive the development of some Western countries and has changed most others—how could it not? It is an exciting, powerful force with the potential to benefit those who move on, those who stay behind and those who receive. But immigration provokes difficulties that cut across party lines and disrupt old coalitions, thus requiring governments to constantly adjust established policies and invent new ones. Involving immigrants themselves is essential to designing any successful strategy, but their incorporation into political decision-making is itself one of the problems to be solved. How political officials and policymakers deal with immigration over the next few decades will be just as important as the question of how they will deal with the movement of money, ideas, goods and boundaries across the continent of Europe.

Further Reading

Bauböck, Rainer (ed.). *Migration and Citizenship: Legal Status, Rights, and Political Participation*. Amsterdam: Amsterdam University Press, 2006.

Bloemraad, Irene. *Becoming a Citizen: Incorporating Immigrants and Refugees in the United States and Canada*. Berkeley, CA: University of California Press, 2006.

Hochschild, Jennifer, and John Mollenkopf (eds.). *The Future of Immigrant Political Incorporation: A Trans-Atlantic Comparison*. Ithaca, NY: Cornell University Press, 2009 (forthcoming).

Joppke, Christian. *Selecting by Origin: Ethnic Migration in the Liberal State*. Cambridge, MA: Harvard University Press, 2005.

Joppke, Christian, and Eva Morawska (eds.). *Toward Assimilation and Citizenship: Immigrants in Liberal Nation-States*. New York: Palgrave Macmillan, 2003.

Kasinitz, Philip, John Mollenkopf, Mary Waters and Jennifer Holdaway. *Inheriting the City: The Children of Immigrants Come of Age*. New York and Cambridge, MA: Russell Sage Foundation and Harvard University Press, 2008.

Klausen, Jytte. *The Islamic Challenge: Politics and Religion in Western Europe*. Oxford: Oxford University Press, 2005.

Koopmans, Ruud, Paul Statham, Marco Giugni and Florence Passy (eds.). *Contested Citizenship: Immigration and Cultural Diversity in Europe*. Minneapolis: University of Minnesota Press, 2005.

Massey, Douglas (ed.). *New Faces in New Places: The Changing Geography of American Immigration*. New York: Russell Sage Foundation, 2008.

Zolberg, Aristide. *A Nation by Design: Immigration Policy in the Fashioning of America*. New York and Cambridge, MA: Russell Sage Foundation and Harvard University Press, 2006.

Part III: Summary of the Discussion

Inaugural Meeting of the Transatlantic Council on Migration

Transatlantic Council on Migration

The inaugural meeting of the Transatlantic Council on Migration took place in Bellagio, Italy from April 21–25. The plenary meeting of the Council focused on citizenship issues, which is the subject of this summary.

This discussion summary aims to provide readers with a record of the deliberations of the Council members and the experts invited to take part in the meeting. Discussions were held under the Chatham House Rule, which seeks to foster openness and information-sharing by assuring speakers that their identities and affiliations will not be linked to their comments during any public characterization of the meeting.

The Role of Citizenship in Our Societies Today

Citizenship policy is critical to the vitality and well-being of societies and immigrant communities alike. But it also presents a minefield because it is by definition enmeshed in delicate questions of identity and belonging. Citizenship dictates who can belong to, and participate in, society as full-fledged members.

The discussion ranged from defining citizenship to valuing its importance. Three essential rights conferred by citizenship stood out: protection against extradition; the value and use of the passport; and the right to vote and participate in elections.

"Citizenship is a crowning of the process of integration [and] the substance of the state."

European Citizenship

The discussion concentrated for some time on the subject of citizenship in the European Union (EU). In Europe, EU citizenship has emerged as a potential solution to overcome some of the pronounced differences between Member States over their individual immigration and integration policies. A number of options were put forward:

- Direct EU citizenship: Imposing standards of European Union citizenship on Member States that would supersede individual national standards.
- Harmonization of citizenship: Permitting Member States to retain their individual citizenship policies but within an EU-wide common standard of access to citizenship,
- Civic citizenship: Recognizing non-EU nationals as equal to EU nationals, but without political rights.

Given the difficult EU legal basis for citizenship and political and policymaking realities, the discussants generally thought the third option to be the most politically feasible. Severing linkages between national and EU citizenship may encourage Member States to maintain strict national laws on citizenship. It may however encourage a federal vision of Europe, which would be unacceptable to many Member States. Harmonization is very unlikely, though it was suggested that a European coordination of citizenship policies is both feasible and advantageous.

Increasingly, European governments are streamlining criteria for naturalization and emphasizing the universal values inherent in citizenship. However, if hurdles to acquiring citizenship are set too high, citizenship reforms will result in less, rather than more, immigrant integration. There is public interest in naturalizing citizens and ensuring that permanent populations have political representation.

The discussants generally agreed that Europe needs to reconsider concepts of *jus soli* (citizenship by birthplace) and citizenship regulations for the children of migrants. Acquisition of nationality should be ensured for the second, third and fourth generations as a matter of course. Naturalization is getting more difficult in some countries and this trend is troubling.

It was noted that there is an opportunity—and also increasingly a rationale—for states to work together to ensure that dual sets of citizenship rights do not conflict. The discussants generally agreed that citizenship should be reconceived as a multi-level phenomenon.

The discussion then focused on the likelihood and shape of citizenship policies. The right to freedom of movement in the Schengen area has created an impetus for harmonization. Nevertheless, most participants thought that harmonization will be promoted by national interests and not by a desire to transfer authority on this issue to the European Union and not as a consequence of free movement.

The discussants thought that there was a risk of a race to the bottom with respect to harmonization. However, if one accepts the principle that citizenship should be given to stakeholders—and only stakeholders—then solid, basic rules should emerge. The EU dimension is important as the differences between Member States are persistent.

Lunch Discussion

"The integration of immigrants, like it or not, is an essential job and not only from the angle of those who are human rights-minded."

Integration is not only an essential job, but a very difficult one.

"Europeans tend to think that if you act on the basis of your political correctness, then politically correct events will occur. Not at all."

Speakers emphasized that integration policies need to be inclusive and cannot be "preached". There is a need for mutual acceptance and common aims for the future. Participants pointed out that in the United States being an American goes beyond national or cultural heritages derived from elsewhere, whether they be Irish, Polish or of some other origin. The question was posed as to whether such a sense of belonging is possible in Europe, where European and national identities exist comfortably together.

The discussants generally agreed that policymakers need to be clear about what they are doing when making citizenship conditional: Are they making the process more restrictive or giving substance to what is already on offer (the rights, duties and benefits of citizenship)? The group differed on the question of how citizenship was to be understood: Is it a step towards integration or the crowning step in a process of integration.

The discussion then focused on the political aspects of citizenship policy. While some countries do not have a quantitative problem with migration, this does not resolve the political barriers to accessing citizenship. In Germany, *jus sanguinis* (citizenship derived by right of blood) has been the principle for a century. Changing the law also requires a change in mindset within societies in general, a change which may not move as quickly as legislation does.

Raising the Bar: Emerging Trends in Citizenship Policy

Participants heard from the experience of a number of experts in different areas of citizenship policy and from different countries.

The discussion began by highlighting the demographic realities of immigration in Europe and North America. For example, 38 percent of the children aged seven or younger in North Rhine-Westphalia were immigrants or the children of immigrants. Such demographic realities ask some very real questions about citizenship.

The session continued with an investigation of case studies in three countries.

The Netherlands

There has been an effort to link citizenship to integration since the 1980s and several approaches have been tried—the integration portfolio has moved through three ministries for instance. The current focus is on sustainable contact between immigrant and host communities.

The current government has approved a plan with civic/active citizenship at its center. One indicator of success was the measured response among Muslim communities to the anti-Islam film "Fitna" by the controversial far-right Dutch politician Gert Wilder.

Sweden

The Swedish approach makes a clear distinction between citizenship and integration. Integration, or common values, is very much a "sister debate". Citizenship is seen narrowly as a set of legal rights and duties.

Most immigrants to Sweden are forced or humanitarian migrants, so they understand the value of democracy.

Norway

A significant rise in immigration has led to challenges of integration. Before 2006, citizenship was based on seven years residence and a good conduct requirement. New legislation in 2006 placed language center-stage: 300 hours of language instruction are now required.

Norway has not, however, introduced either a language test or a civic test for citizenship because of concerns that they may prove to be a barrier to naturalization.

Cross-Country Trends

The discussion then switched focus from country trends to cross-country trends. There was a robust debate as to whether language and other types of tests and requirements added value to citizenship. Several lines were drawn:

- Some felt that language and other types of training should be "front-loaded" in the citizenship process as language in particular was crucial to integration success.
- Others suggested this may have a deterrent effect and, if taken to its logical conclusion, would result in pre-immigration requirements. This latter point was variously described as "cruel" and "legitimate".

There was also agreement among the Council interlocutors on several key points:

- Citizenship policy should foster a sense of belonging to a population.
- Citizenship tests, if they are introduced, should never be a punitive measure intended to exclude.
- Citizenship is a core human right and provides instrumental protections that differ from being "integrated".

Several participants referred to being clear about the goal of policy. Put another way, what is it that we are trying to achieve? Is it, for example, to increase integration, to attract labor or to change the views of the settled groups in society?

Other participants made a related point about how the costs and benefits of citizenship were distributed. The long-term political negotiations are concerned with costs and benefits, and with accommodating racial, ethnic and religious groups. Essentially, when does privilege for newcomers "click in" and how can we calibrate pressures on both sides, i.e. the sides of the immigrant and the native-born?

Throughout the discussion, cautions were given that "citizenship is not just immigrant integration". Governments cannot rely on citizenship policy for achieving integration—integration is perhaps best viewed as a continuum, on which citizenship is one point on the arc.

"Citizenship can be useful but if you don't activate integration ... it is just a formal right."

Designing Policies to Encourage Participation

The session began with a discussion of the cross-cutting political and public pressures that complicate the immigration and integration debates. Nevertheless, participants noted that on the issue of integration an increasing common ground between parties of the left and the right is being found.

Some discussants questioned whether governments are flexible enough to deliver effective language and other integration services and to respond to shifting migration trends. Integration efforts have been far more successful in the private sector and in civil society.

"It may be we have seen the problem and the problem is us."

Though governments have stepped up their language programs and the funding for those programs, the process of ensuring full participation rests on far more than language. Whether immigrants feel they are treated fairly and as fully participating members of the society, or not, is a crucial factor in integration.

"Language alone is not the solution for the problem, nor is citizenship."

Participants discussed the importance of:
- Offering orientation courses for newcomers to explain the culture and values of their new country.
- Early contact between the host society and the immigrant, beginning first with language training and then expanding to work training and recognition of foreign credentials and work experience.

157

- Creating a two-way street in integration, namely by providing the conditions in which immigrants will feel comfortable about participating in the broader society while, at the same time, urging them to take steps to integrate.
- Ensuring a clear consensus on the meaning of citizenship and assuring newcomers that there is no such thing as conditional citizenship.

There was also discussion that integration policies should not be aimed uniquely at immigrants. There is a broader societal participation problem in lower socioeconomic classes that can result in some native-born residents resenting newcomers if they feel their socio-economic status might worsen due to new competition for jobs. The Council discussed at length the question of whether integration policies should be targeted at immigrants or made universal, with some specific components aimed at migrants.

In some cases, integration programs that once identified and targeted funding based on students' ethnic origin instead now examine their parents' socio-economic status.

"We need to color-code the solution, not the analysis."

Essential Elements of a Path to Citizenship

What is the best narrative for creating a path to citizenship, and are multiple paths in fact preferable? Whatever the case may be, the path chosen has to be acceptable to all members of society, i.e. to both migrants and non-migrants.

When looking at citizenship and integration, there is a tendency to focus solely upon the groups which have trouble integrating and forget all those who are well integrated. One-sided information is thus presented to the public, which in turn creates negative stereotypes. There is a need to create bridges between civil society and the public at the local level, bringing together all those acting to promote integration, including the business sector. Institutions need to be open to this. Citizenship is not just about rights, but also about legal status and equality.

It was suggested that sending countries' increasing efforts to renew or strengthen ties with their citizens living abroad might distract from immigrants' integration and their desire to focus primarily on life in their new country. Others disagreed and noted that a diaspora identity can be an asset and that often it is the best integrated immigrants who are able to play important roles both in their countries of birth and choice. Participants considered whether the concept of circular or temporary migration may have a negative effect on the status of longer-term migrants and settlers in a country, thus lessening their willingness to integrate.

Migration is not just concerned with the receiving country and policymakers would do well to remember this. Migrants can be transnationally active in more than one community and governments should accommodate this fact. Similarly, citizenship should be able to accommodate the concepts of "return" and "movements back and forth".

There needs to be a stronger focus upon what binds us together—civic nationalism—and the concept of neighborliness. Finding a common identity, however, can be difficult, because this may mean different things at different levels: nationally, regionally, locally. Indeed, cities in Europe are pushing European integration policies forward.

It was noted that a focus on citizenship per se, may be misleading. Instead, integration takes place through the provision of housing, spatial planning and the local environment. However, some recognized that there is a transatlantic divide when discussing politics and common identity: individualism defines life in the United States in a way which is not so prevalent in Europe. Whereas in the United States, 'self-made' is an established concept, in Europe, society is responsible for success. Some questions were put to the group:

- What should be the defining instruments of citizenship?
- What requirements might reasonably be imposed?
- What voting rights should be offered and when?
- What are the responsibilities of civic society itself?

The conversation briefly touched upon voting rights and local voting was generally perceived to be uncontentious and positive. The role of language was highlighted and the need to return to the practicalities of language as a skill rather than just a symbol of integration.

There was a brief debate concerning how much can be asked of immigrants: essentially, are we demanding more from immigrants than from citizens? Some suggested that civic responsibilities have to be available to all, but at a price. Others noted that the expectations of new citizens to become politically involved can be overemphasized: not everyone has to get elected.

In terms of a path to citizenship, several participants noted that it is difficult to define a clear way. Instead a 'flexible toolbox' was proposed, with differentiated yet inclusive options. Citizenship is not the most important tool in the toolbox: labor market participation and education are both vital factors for integration. Without these, even citizens remain isolated. Similarly, a civic identity which is too strong can suppress other identities and lead to isolation.

Some conclusions were drawn at the end of the discussion:

- Citizenship pathways are more about solidarity and cohesion than selectivity and exclusion. While the destination may be the same, there are different roads leading to it.
- There are national principles for defining citizenship in a polity, but some local expression is also necessary.
- There are broader components of citizenship—such as work, culture, access to justice—which should not be forgotten.
- There needs to be more consideration of what governments and the community should be providing: language and citizenship classes, access to work or education.
- The pathway needs to be clearly marked by earned stages.

Governments need to provide channels and pathways, but one must remember that states have developed their own citizenship logic dating back hundreds of years. These ideas are not easy to change.

Biographies of the Council Members and Staff

Council Members

Giuliano Amato was Italy's Minister of the Interior in Romano Prodi's government from 2006 through spring 2008 and served twice as Prime Minister, first from 1992 to 1993 and then from 2000 to 2001. Minister Amato was more recently Vice President of the Convention on the Future of Europe, with former Belgian Prime Minister Jean-Luc Dehaene, that drafted the European Constitution and headed the Amato group. Minister Amato was a member of the senate representing the constituency of Grosseto in Tuscany from 2001 to 2006 and served as a member of parliament from 1983 to 1993. He was Undersecretary of State to the Prime Minister's office from 1983 to 1987, Deputy Prime Minister and Finance Minister from 1987 to 1988 and again Finance Minister from 1988 to 1989, a position he briefly returned to in 1999. He also was a university professor in constitutional matters and was Chairman of the Antitrust Authority from 1994 to 1997. Minister Amato received a first degree in law from the University of Pisa and a master's degree in comparative law from Columbia University.

Xavier Becerra represents California's 31st District (contained within the city of Los Angeles) in the US House of Representatives. The Democrat is Assistant House Speaker, a position that allows him to help set leadership priorities and drive the legislative decision-making process. First elected to Congress in 1992, Rep. Becerra is a member of the Congressional Hispanic Caucus, where he served as Chairman during the 105th Congress (1997–98). The Congressman is also a member of the Executive Committee of the Congressional Asian Pacific American Caucus. At the international level, he serves as Vice Chairman of the U.S.-Korea Interparliamentary Exchange and is Co-Chair of the Congressional Friends of Spain Caucus. Rep. Becerra earned his bachelor's and law degrees from Stanford University.

Mel Cappe began his term as President of the Institute for Research on Public Policy (IRPP) on June 1, 2006. Prior to joining IRPP, Mr. Cappe spent more than 30 years in Canadian public service, most recently as the High Commissioner for Canada to the United Kingdom of Great Britain and Northern Ireland. Prior to that, he was Canada's top public servant as Clerk of the Privy Council, Secretary to the Cabinet and Head of the Public Service in January 1999, a position he relinquished in May 2002 to become Special Advisor to Prime Minister Jean Chrétien. He has also held senior economic and policy positions in federal government departments in Ottawa, including the Treasury Board, Department of Finance and Consumer and Corporate Affairs. He has served as Deputy Secretary to the Treasury Board, Deputy Minister of the Environment, Deputy Minister of Human Resources Development, Deputy Minister of Labor and Chairman of the Employment Insurance Commission. Mr. Cappe has a master's degree in economics from the University of Western Ontario and did doctoral studies at the University of Toronto.

Armin Laschet has been the Minister for Inter-Generation and Family Affairs, Women and Integration of North Rhine-Westphalia since 2005. He is also the Chairman of the Federal Committee for International Cooperation and Human Rights of the CDU Germany, an Executive Member of the European People's Party (EPP), Treasurer of the Christian Democrat International (CDI) and President of the CDU District Association, Aachen. From 1999 to 2005, he was a Member of the European Parliament; from 1994 to 1998, he was a Member of the German Bundestag; and from 1989 to 2004, he was a member of the Aachen City Council. He has also worked as the Editor-in-Chief and President and CEO of the publishing house Einhard Verlag; as

Scientific Advisor to Rita Süssmuth (former President of the German Bundestag); and as a freelance reporter for Bavarian radio stations and Bavarian television. He is an Associate Lecturer of European Studies at RWTH Aachen (Aachen University of Technology). Minister Laschet studied law and political science in Munich and Bonn, received a 1st state in his examination in law before the Higher Regional Court of Cologne and studied journalism.

Libe Rieber-Mohn is the State Secretary for integration, immigration and diversity matters in the Norwegian Ministry of Labor and Inclusion. From 2004 to 2005, State Secretary Rieber-Mohn served as a political advisor for the Labor Party Parliamentary Group. Before that she held various positions in the Gamle Oslo District in the municipality of Oslo, including Project Director, Head of Section and City Government Secretary. Additionally, she has worked as a Senior Consultant at Cap Germini Ernst & Young and as a Research Fellow at the Institute for Social Research. State Secretary Rieber-Mohn has also been Chair of the Labor Party's Immigration and Integration Committee (2004) and a member of the Oslo City Council (1988–92). She holds a master's in sociology from the University of Oslo and did coursework at the Harvard Extension School.

Ana Palacio is the Senior Vice President for International Affairs and Marketing for AREVA, the world's largest nuclear energy company. Ms. Palacio was a member of the Spanish Parliament, former Foreign Minister of Spain and a member of Carnegie Corporation's Board of Trustees from December 2005. Ms. Palacio was a member of the European Parliament during the 4th and 5th parliamentary terms (1994–2002), where she chaired the Legal Affairs and Internal Market Committee and the Justice and Home Affairs Committee and was elected by her peers to chair the Parliament's Conference of Committee Chairmen, the senior body for coordinating legislative work. Most recently, she has been the Senior Vice President and General Counsel for the World Bank. A lawyer by profession, Ms. Palacio is a member and past Executive President of the Academy of European Law. She has held senior positions in the governing body of European lawyers and is an honorary member of the Bar of England and Wales. She is also a member of the faculty of the European College in Parma, Italy. She is a member of the international advisory boards of both the Council on Foreign Relations and the Instituto de Empresa Business School in Madrid, and is a member of the governing boards for both the Fundación Española del Instituto Weizmann de Israel and the Fundación para el Análisis y los Estudios Sociales in Madrid. She holds degrees in law, political science and sociology.

Since 2006, *Trevor Phillips* has been chairman of the new Equality and Human Rights Commission, which took over the work of Britain's three existing equality commissions. A journalist, broadcaster and television industry executive, Mr. Phillips was elected as a member of the Greater London Authority in May 2000 and became Chair of the Assembly later that month. He is also co-founder of the Equate Organization, a social change consultancy, and is Director of Pepper Productions. He was executive producer of "Windrush" (which won the Royal Television Society Documentary Series of the Year award in 1998), "Britain's Slave Trade", "Second Chance" and "When Black Became Beautiful". He is a Vice President of the Royal Television Society. He is a board member of the Almeida Theatre in Islington, Aldeburgh Productions and the Bernie Grant Center in Tottenham, and is a patron of the Sickle Cell Society. Between 1993 and 1998, he was chair of the Runnymede Trust. In addition to many newspaper articles and comment pieces, Mr. Phillips was co-author (with Mike Phillips) of "Windrush: The Irresistible Rise of Multiracial Britain", published in 1998 and co-author (with S.I. Martin) of "Britain's Slave Trade", published the following year. He studied chemistry at Imperial College London.

Rita Süssmuth is former President of the German Federal Parliament and former Federal Minister for Family Affairs, Women, Youth and Health. In 2006, Dr. Süssmuth became the Chair of the European Union's High-Level Group on Social Integration of Ethnic Minorities and their full Participation in the Labor Market. In 2006, she joined the Advisory Board of the Development Center Project "Gaining from Migration" of the Organization for Economic Cooperation and Development. She was member of the Global Commission on International Migration, which presented a report to Kofi Annan in October 2005 entitled "Migration in an Interconnected World: New Directions for Action". She is the President of the OTA-University in Berlin. From May 2003 until December 2004, Dr. Süssmuth was appointed by the German Government as Chair of the Independent Council of Experts on Migration and Integration. She is also a member of the Steering Committee for "Intercultural Conflict and Societal Integration" at the Social Science Research Center Berlin and holds a series of other assignments and memberships with national and international bodies. From 2000 to 2001, Dr. Süssmuth presided over the Independent Commission on Migration to Germany which resulted in the report on "Steering Migration and Fostering Integration" (July 2001). Dr. Süssmuth has a long distinguished political and academic career. She held several senior positions, including Vice President of the Organization for Security and Cooperation in Europe Parliamentary Assembly and was a Member of the German Federal Parliament. She has also been Director of the Research Institute "Woman and Society" and Professor of International Comparative Educational Science at the Universities of Bochum and Dortmund. Dr. Süssmuth completed her studies in romance languages at the Universities of Münster, Tübingen and Paris, and received a Ph.D. in education, sociology and psychology.

Antonio Vitorino, a Partner of Gonçalves Pereira, Castelo Branco & Associados, is the former European Commissioner for Justice and Home Affairs (1999–2004). He served as Portugal's Deputy Prime Minister and Minister of Defense from 1995 to 1997, and prior to that he was a Member of the European Parliament (1994–95). He has also been a Judge of the Portuguese Constitutional Court (1989–94), Vice President of Portugal Telecom Internacional (1998–99) and Secretary of State of the Government of Macau (1986–87). He has been an assistant professor at the University of Lisbon Law School since 1982 and has also taught as a professor at the Universidade Autónoma Luís de Camões and Universidade Internacional of Lisbon. Mr. Vitorino is a member of the Portuguese Bar Association and the author of several works on constitutional law, political science and community law, both in Portugal and abroad. He holds a master's in legal and political science and received his law degree from the University of Lisbon Law School.

Council Guests

Edward Greenspon took over as Editor-in-Chief of *The Globe and Mail* in July 2002 after 16 years with the paper. Previously, he was Political Editor of *The Globe and Mail*, writing a thrice-weekly column from Ottawa and co-hosting CTV's weekly current affairs program, "Question Period". From 1999 to 2000, he served as Executive Editor. Mr. Greenspon began his career as a journalist at the *Lloydminster Times* and also worked for the *Regina Leader-Post* and *Financial Post*. He started at The Globe as a business reporter specializing in media industries. He later served as the paper's first European business correspondent in the late 1980s and early 1990s. He covered the economic integration of Europe and took an early interest in globalization. Upon returning to Canada, he worked as Managing Editor of *Report on Business* and Deputy Managing Editor of the entire newspaper before taking up the duties of Ottawa bureau chief in 1993. He is the winner of the 2002 Hyman Solomon Award for excellence in public policy journalism. His book "Double Vision: The Inside Story of the Liberals in Power" was a co-winner of the 1996 Douglas Purvis Award for the best piece of policy writing in Canada. In 2001, he and pollster Darrell Bricker published "Searching for Certainty: Inside the New Canadian Mindset". Mr. Greenspon has an honors degree in journalism and political science from Carleton University in Ottawa. He was a Commonwealth Scholar at the London School of Economics, where he earned a master's degree in politics and government.

Christer Hallerby has been State Secretary of Sweden's Ministry of Integration and Gender Equality since October 2006. Apart from integration and gender equality issues, the Ministry is also responsible for metropolitan affairs, democracy and human rights, anti-discrimination policy, minority policy, youth policy, popular movement policy and consumer policy. Immediately prior to this appointment, Mr. Hallerby ran his own consultancy company that worked on strategic development from a business intelligence perspective. He also has worked as Deputy CEO with responsibility for consultancy at Docere Intelligence AB and as Deputy CEO and head of the business intelligence section of TEMO AB (a company for market research and opinion polls). Between 1994 and 1999, Mr. Hallerby was a co-owner, partner and senior consultant of a firm of management consultants. He was primarily specialized in scenario planning, business intelligence and industrial analysis, and value-creating processes in companies and the public sector. Other political appointments that he has held include State Secretary responsible for refugee and immigrant issues; Deputy Secretary General of the Liberal Party and head of the political and international departments; Political Secretary/Research Officer at the National Organization of the Liberal Party; Special Advisor at the Ministry of the Labor Market and Industry; Political Secretary/Research Officer at the National Organization of the Liberal Party; and Political Advisor at the Prime Minister's Office. State Secretary Hallerby also served in the military, studied industrial economics at Linköping Institute of Technology and studied business economics and political science at Stockholm University.

Guido Lenzi most recently served as the Diplomatic Adviser to the Minister of the Interior in Italy During his career, he has served in a number of other positions, including the Political Directorate of the Foreign Ministry in 2004, as a permanent representative to the Organization for Security and Cooperation in Europe (OSCE) in Vienna in 2000 and as Director of the WEU Institute for Security Studies in Paris in 1995. His postings abroad included London, Moscow and the United Nations. He also served as the Diplomatic Adviser to the

President of the Senate in 1994, the Deputy Head of Cabinet for the Foreign Minister and the Minister of Defense, as well as the head of the NATO desk in the Foreign Ministry. Mr. Lenzi, an Italian citizen, entered the Foreign Service in 1964. He graduated with a degree in law from the University of Florence in 1963.

Gregory Rodriguez is a columnist for the *Los Angeles Times* and Director of the California Fellows Program and Irvine Senior Fellow at the New America Foundation. He has written widely on issues of national identity, social cohesion, assimilation, race relations, religion, immigration, ethnicity, demographics and social and political trends in such leading publications as *The New York Times, The Wall Street Journal, The Economist, The Washington Post* and the *Los Angeles Times,* where he is an op-ed columnist. Mr. Rodriguez is the author of "Mongrels, Bastards, Orphans and Vagabonds: Mexican Immigration and the Future of Race in America" (Pantheon, 2007).

Council Management and Staff

Thor Arne Aass is the Director General of the Department of Migration in the Norwegian Ministry of Labor and Inclusion. He has been in managerial positions in the Department of Migration since 1990, as Director General since 1996, and has followed the Department of Migration through reorganizations between various ministries. Mr. Aass advises Norwegian state secretaries and parliamentarians on all migration matters, immigration and refugee issues, as well as integration issues. From 1988 through 1990, Mr. Aass was Senior Executive Officer in the Department of Migration. Before entering the Ministry, Mr. Aass worked as Executive and Senior Executive Officer for the Directorate of Telecommunication. From 2005 through 2006, Mr. Aass served as Chair for the Working Group on Resettlement, consisting of UNHCR and the governments offering resettlement on a regular basis. From 2004 through 2005, Mr. Aass served as Chair for the Inter-Governmental Consultations on Asylum, Refugee and Migration

Policies (IGC) Working Group on Return. From 2003 through 2004, Mr. Aass served as Chair for the IGC. Mr. Aass received an M.A. in political science from the University of Oslo in 1984. In 2006, he was a Visiting Fellow to the Migration Policy Institute.

Barbro Birgitta Appelqvist Bakken is the Director General, Department of Integration and Diversity, Ministry of Labor and Inclusion. In her current position, she serves as an advisor on integration issues to State Secretary Rieber-Mohn. Prior to that, she served as Assistant Director General, Deputy Director General and Director General in the Department of Immigration, Ministry of Local Government and Regional Development. Ms. Bakken has worked at various levels of the Norwegian government. From 1985 to 1992, she worked in the central administration in the Municipality of Oslo. Before that she worked as the General Manager and Departmental Manager at the Immigrant Office for Oslo. She also worked in the social security and rehabilitation departments in the Trosterud practice center in Oslo. She received her degree in social work from the University of Ørebro, Sweden

Elizabeth Collett is a policy analyst at the European Policy Centre, an independent Brussels-based policy think tank that is policy partner with the Transatlantic Council on Migration. Ms. Collett coordinates the Migration and Integration Forum at the EPC, which is run in collaboration with the King Baudouin Foundation. Previously, she worked for the International Organization for Migration in Geneva and for the Institute for the Study of International Migration in Washington, DC. Her publications include "Legal Review on Trafficking in Persons in the Caribbean" (IOM, 2005), "One size fits all? The need for tailored integration policies for migrants in the European Union" (EPC, 2006) and "Making migration work: the role of employers in migrant integration" (with Karolina Sitek, EPC, 2008). She has contributed chapters to a number of publications including "Managing Migration in Ireland: An Economic and Social Analysis" (IOM, 2006), "Rethinking Immigration and Integration: A New Centre-Left Agenda" (Policy Network 2007), "Think Global, Act European" (Notre Europe, 2008), as well as articles for *Challenge Europe* and *International Migration*. She has a law degree from Oxford University and a master's in foreign service from Georgetown University.

Brian C. Grant has held the position of Director General of International and Intergovernmental Relations at Citizenship and Immigration Canada (CIC) since July 2005. In this capacity he has led responsibility for Canada's engagement on international migration issues at bilateral, regional and multilateral forums. He has also led responsibility for CIC's relations with provincial and territorial governments in Canada, which share jurisdiction over immigration under the Canadian Constitution. Mr. Grant also has responsibility for relations with municipalities and other stakeholders in Canada who are increasingly becoming involved in immigration issues. Prior to July 2005, Mr. Grant was the Director General of Strategic Policy and Partnerships, CIC. From February 1999 to July 2001, Mr. Grant worked for the United Kingdom Immigration Service (the Home Office) in London as part of an exchange of senior immigration officials between Canada and the United Kingdom. From 1990 to 1999, Mr. Grant held a number of positions within the enforcement area of CIC including Director of Control and Enforcement Policy, Director of Program Development and Acting Director General of Enforcement. He was lead negotiator for Canada on the migration chapter of the North American Free Trade Agreement and has had extensive experience in revising immigration legislation and regulations. Mr. Grant began his public service career in 1984 as an information officer with Employment and Immigration Canada. He holds a bachelor's from Carleton University and a master's from the University of Leeds.

Marilyn Haimé is the Director of Citizenship and Integration at the Ministry of Housing, Spatial Planning and the Environment in the Netherlands. Before this she was Director of the Minorities Integration Policy Directorate at the Ministry of Justice. Ms. Haimé came from the Ministry of Internal Affairs and Kingdom Relations, where she started her career in the civil service as a legal policy officer in the Police Directorate. She subsequently transferred to the Constitutional Affairs and Legislation Directorate, where she dealt with a wide range of subjects related to constitutional law, including the Law on Equal Treatment, the constitutional rights of civil servants and the Passport Law. In addition, Ms. Haimé was involved in the development of legislation and in constitutional affairs related to legal protection (National Ombudsman, Council of State, right of complaint) and general rules of administrative law (Secretary of the Commission on General Rule of Administrative Law). Prior to her current position, Ms. Haimé was Adjunct Director of the Constitutional Affairs and Legislation Directorate and Project Manager on Referendum Legislation. She began her career as the coordinator of the Victims Support Project in Rotterdam. Ms. Haimé has also held administrative positions in a number of organizations, including the Dutch Lawyers Association for Human Rights; the Association for Administrative Law; Meander, an organization for intercultural development. She is currently a commissioner at the Foundation Humanitas in Rotterdam. Ms. Haimé was born in Surinam, completed her secondary education in the Netherlands and graduated from Erasmus University in Rotterdam where she majored in criminal and private law.

Gregory A. Maniatis oversees the European programs for the Migration Policy Institute (MPI) and serves as Executive Director of the Transatlantic Council on Migration. He is also advisor to Peter Sutherland, the United Nations Special Representative for Migration. Mr. Maniatis consults with the European Commission, Member-State governments, the European Parliament and international organizations on all aspects of immigration and integration policy. In 2007, he led MPI's advisory work for the EU Presidencies of Germany and Portugal; in previous years, he had overseen MPI's work with the EU Presidencies of Greece and the Netherlands. Prior to his positions at MPI and the UN, Mr. Maniatis was founder and publisher of the magazine *Odyssey*, an English-language bimonthly that is the leading international magazine on Greece and Greeks around the world.

He is also a writer and producer whose reportage and commentary have been featured in the *International Herald Tribune, The Wall Street Journal, New York* magazine, *The Washington Monthly,* PBS Television and many other media outlets. Mr. Maniatis is a graduate of Princeton University's Woodrow Wilson School of Public and International Affairs and a recipient of a *certificat* from the Institut d'Etudes Politiques in Paris. He is a Member of the Council on Foreign Relations.

Geri Mannion is Director of Carnegie Corporation's US Democracy Program and Special Opportunities Fund. She has chaired the US Democracy Program since 1998, after staffing the Corporation's program of Special Projects for almost ten years. In addition to supporting projects that focus on improving broad civic engagement, the program focuses on immigrant civic integration, youth civic education and election administration. As Director of the Corporation's Special Opportunities Fund, Ms. Mannion oversees the Corporation's response to proposals that are important but not related to the foundation's primary foci. Ms. Mannion has spent more than 30 years in the field of philanthropy, working at both the Rockefeller and Ford Foundations before joining Carnegie. At the Rockefeller Foundation, where she spent 13 years in a variety of positions, she became a program associate in the international relations program. At the Ford Foundation, Ms. Mannion consulted with its international affairs program—assisting with both grant evaluation and grant-making—in its focus on arms control and security issues. Active in professional organizations, Ms. Mannion is a leader in the Funders' Committee for Citizen Participation, an affinity group of funders that encourages foundations to fund voter registration, voting rights, civic education and campaign finance reform. Ms. Mannion holds a bachelor's degree in English and a master's in political science from Fordham University.

Michelle Mittelstadt is Director of Communications for the Migration Policy Institute, and is responsible for developing and implementing MPI's strategic communications, managing the websites and publications and coordinating the Institute's media outreach and events.

A veteran journalist, she joined MPI in February 2008 after covering immigration policy, Congress and border-related issues since the early 1990s in the Washington bureaus of *The Associated Press, The Dallas Morning News* and *The Houston Chronicle*. She has written hundreds of articles examining US immigration policy, border and interior enforcement, and the post-9/11 legislative and executive branch changes that have altered the immigration landscape. She also covered the Departments of Justice and Homeland Security. Before coming to Washington, Ms. Mittelstadt was an editor with *The Associated Press* in Dallas and the managing editor of *The Courier Herald* in Dublin, Ga. She holds a bachelor's in journalism from the University of Georgia.

Christal Morehouse is currently Program Manager for the Bertelsmann Stiftung in the field of migration and integration. She is responsible for managing the Stiftung's integration programs at the European and transatlantic levels. From January to December 2006 she was the Head of Office for Prof. Dr. Rita Süssmuth, the former President of the German Bundestag. Between January and December 2005 she conducted research for the Global Commission on International Migration as a German member of the staff of the Commission. From June 2003 until December 2004, she was part of the research team of the German Independent Council of Experts on Migration and Integration in Berlin. Ms. Morehouse has advised various European and American multinational institutions on policy matters. She was among the experts whose advice on integration issues was sought by the German EU Presidency in 2007. In 2004, she was a consultant to the Organization of American States for anti-trafficking research in Europe. Her publications include contributions to the following books: "Migration und Integration gestalten: Transatlantische Impulse für globale Herausforderungen" (Verlag Bertelsmann Stiftung, 2008), "Integration braucht faire Bildungschancen" (Verlag Bertelsmann Stiftung, 2008) and "Immigrant Students Can Succeed: Lessons from around the Globe (Verlag Bertelsmann Stiftung, 2008). Ms. Morehouse is currently completing a Ph.D. in political science at the Humboldt University in Berlin. She holds a master's degree in political science from the Free University in Berlin and a B.A. from Wittenberg University in Ohio. She was a Fulbright Scholar.

Monica A. SanMiguel is a Research Associate at the Rockefeller Foundation. Prior to her position at Rockefeller, Ms. SanMiguel worked as a Research Assistant at the Council of State Governments and a Research Assistant at the University of California at Los Angeles's International Institute—Latin America Center. Ms. SanMiguel held a Public Policy & International Affairs Fellowship at Princeton University and earned her bachelor's degree in international development studies at the University of California, Los Angeles.

Will Somerville is a Senior Policy Analyst at the Migration Policy Institute. Prior to joining MPI, Will Somerville worked as a Senior Policy Officer at the Commission for Racial Equality, where he led on asylum and immigration policy; as a Policy and Research Manager at the Center for Economic and Social Inclusion; as a Policy Analyst at the Prime Minister's Strategy Unit, Cabinet Office; and as a researcher for the Institute for Public Policy Research (ippr). He has managed over 20 research and consultancy projects and has over 20 publications to his credit. His publications include "Reinventing the Public Employment Service: The Changing Role of Employment Assistance in Great Britain and Germany" (Anglo-German Foundation, 2004) and "The Integration of Refugees and New Migrants" (Home Office, 2006) as well as articles for the *Journal of Local Economy*, the *Industrial Relations Services Employment Review* and *Working Brief*. He has also edited five welfare-rights and best-practice books, the latest being "Working in the UK: Second Edition of the Newcomer's Handbook" (CESI, 2006). His most recent sole-authored, peer-reviewed book is "Immigration under New Labour", which was published by the Policy Press in September 2007. He has a first-class degree in history from the University of Leeds and a master's in social policy and planning (awarded with distinction) from the London School of Economics and Political Science.

Alexandros Zavos is President of the Hellenic Migration Policy Institute (IMEPO), a position he has held since April 2004. IMEPO's mission is to research into and understand the phenomenon of migration, and to conduct studies which contribute to the design and implementation of a viable and realistic immigration policy within the EU's framework. In addition, IMEPO acts as the advisor to the Greek government on migration policy issues. In his role as President of IMEPO, Mr. Zavos is involved in the planning and organization of the "Global Forum on Migration and Development", to be held in Greece towards the end of 2009. He is also a mathematician with 27 years of experience in the field of education. He holds a master's degree in mathematics and is a doctoral candidate at the University of Athens. He has also served as Special Advisor to the Greek Minister of Education and has been very active in trade unions in Greece.

Authors

Rainer Bauböck (Council Guest) holds a chair in social and political theory at the Department of Political and Social Sciences of the European University Institute. He is also Vice Chair of the Austrian Academy of Sciences' Commission for Migration and Integration Research. Dr. Bauböck is the author of "Transnational Citizenship: Membership and Rights in International Migration" (1994) and editor of a series of books on migration, citizenship and diversity. In November 2006, he was awarded the Latsis Prize of the European Science Foundation for his work on immigration and social cohesion in modern societies. He received a doctorate in sociology from the University of Vienna.

Thomas Faist is Professor of Transnational Relations and Sociology of Development at the Department of Sociology, Bielefeld University (www.comcad-bielefeld.de). He received his Ph.D. from The Graduate Faculty, New School for Social Research. His research focuses on migration, citizenship and social & development policies. Thomas Faist was Willy-Brandt Guest Professor at the University of Malmö and DAAD Visiting Professor at the University of Toronto. He is the deputy editor of *The Sociological Quarterly*. His recent book publications include "Dual Citizenship in Europe: From Nationhood to Societal Integration" (Ashgate 2007), "Citizenship: Discourse, Theory and Transnational Prospects" (with Peter Kivisto, Blackwell, 2007) and "Dual Citizenship in a Globalizing World: From Unitary to Multiple Citizenship" (Palgrave Macmillan, 2007).

Jürgen Gerdes is a political scientist and a researcher associated with the Center on Migration, Citizenship and Development (COMCAD) at Bielefeld University in Germany. He is currently working in a research project on "Transnationalization, Migration and Transformation: Multi-Level Analysis of Migrant Transnationalism" (TRANS-NET, 7th Framework Programme of the EU).

Kees Groenendijk is Professor of Sociology of Law at the University of Nijmegen, The Netherlands, and Chairman of its Center for Migration Law. He has taught courses on Dutch, European and international migration law since 1975. Dr. Groenendijk is Chairman of the Standing Committee of Experts on international immigration, refugee and criminal law, known as the Meijers Committee. He served as Dean of the Faculty of Law from 1993 to 1995 and was a founding editor of *Rechtspraak Vreemdelingenrecht*, a yearbook on Dutch and international case law on immigration, refugees and race relations. Dr. Groenendijk holds a law degree from the University of Utrecht and did his doctoral thesis on collective interests in civil courts.

Randall A. Hansen (Council Guest) is an Associate Professor of Political Science and holds a Research Chair at the University of Toronto. Previously, he was elected to a Research Fellowship at Christ Church (Oxford), a tutorial fellowship at Merton College (Oxford) and an established Chair in Politics at the University of Newcastle. His current projects include work on immigration and integration in Europe and North America, a book on the bombing of Germany during World War II, and a collaborative project with Desmond King on eugenics and forced sterilization. He is principal investigator on a study of the global governance of migration (with Frank Lazco and Jobst Koehler of the International Organization for Migration). Professor Hansen has held sabbatical fellowships at the Institut des Etudes Politiques, Paris, Humboldt University and Wissenschaftszentrum, Berlin, Trinity College, Dublin, and the University of California, Los Angeles. He is the author of Citizenship and Immigration in Postwar Britain (Oxford University Press, 2000) and has published numerous articles and book chapters on immigration, citizenship and the history of eugenics and forced sterilization. He has a master's degree and a doctorate from the University of Oxford, where he was a Commonwealth Scholar.

Annette Heuser (Council Management) is the Executive Director of the Bertelsmann Foundation North America in Washington, DC, Bertelsmann's newly opened first office in the United States. Prior to this she was Executive Director the Bertelsmann Stiftung in Brussels, which she built up in 2000. From 1995 to summer 2000, she was Director Europe/USA at the Bertelsmann Stiftung in Gütersloh. In this function she was responsible for the management of the European and transatlantic projects and the development of the European networking activities. Before she joined the Bertelsmann Stiftung, she was the editor of the *Jahrbuch der Europäischen Integration*, an annual publication which deals with institutional and political developments within the process of European integration. From 1992 to 1995, she was staff member at the University of Mainz of the Research Group on European Affairs, which is now located at the University of Munich.

Jennifer L. Hochschild (Council Guest) joined the Government Department at Harvard in January 2001, and is now the Henry LaBarre Jayne Professor of Government and Professor of African and African American Studies. She also holds lectureships in the Kennedy School of Government and the Graduate School of Education. Professor Hochschild studies the intersection of American politics and political philosophy—particularly in the areas of race, ethnicity and immigration—and educational policy. She also works on issues in public opinion and political culture. She is the co-author of "The American Dream and the Public Schools" (Oxford University Press, 2003); and author of "Facing Up to the American Dream: Race, Class and the Soul of the Nation" (Princeton University Press, 1995); and "What's Fair? American Beliefs about Distributive Justice" (Harvard University Press, 1981). She is also a co-author or co-editor of other books and articles. Her current project is tentatively entitled "Blurring Racial Boundaries: Skin Color Hierarchy and Multiracialism in American Politics". Professor Hochschild is the founding editor of *Perspectives on Politics*, published by the American Political Science Association. She is also a Fellow of the American Academy of Arts and Sciences, a former vice president of the American Political Science Association, a member of the Board of Trustees of the Russell Sage Foundation and a former member of the Board of Overseers of the General Social Survey. Professor Hochschild taught at Duke University and Columbia University before going to Princeton in 1981.

Hans Martens is Chief Executive of The European Policy Centre (a Brussels-based think tank set up to promote European integration) a position he took up in 2002. Born in Denmark, Hans Martens studied at Aarhus University, specializing in EU affairs and in public administration, and went on to become associate professor in international political and economic relations. In 1979, he joined the Danish Savings Bank Association as Editor-in-Chief and Head of Information. From 1982 to1985 he was Head of the International Department of a Danish trade union (the Salaried Employees' Federation), where he took charge of the organization's international relations, including relations with the OECD and the ILO. In 1985, Hans Martens joined the Copenhagen Handelsbank as Head of the Economic Department and later as Head of the International Private Banking Department. In 1989, he set up Martens International Consulting, specializing in international consultancy and customized training (including in EU affairs) for a number of major companies. Previously a visiting professor at the Universities of Aarhus and Copenhagen, he is a regular lecturer at the Executive MBA Program at Virginia Commonwealth University and a number of European business schools. He leads the vation, reform of public administration), as well as on e-business and e-government. He is the author of a number of books and articles on public administration, European integration, monetary affairs and business strategies for the European market.

John Mollenkopf is Director of the Center for Urban Research at the Graduate Center, City University of New York. He is a Distinguished Professor of Political Science and Sociology at the Graduate Center and coordinates its interdisciplinary concentration in public policy and urban studies. He has authored or edited 15 books on urban politics, urban policy, immigration and New York City. Prior to joining the Graduate Center in 1981, he directed the Economic Development Division of the New York City Department of City Planning and taught urban studies and public management at Stanford University. With Philip Kasinitz, Mary Waters and Jennifer Holdaway, Dr. Mollenkopf recently completed "Inheriting the City", a study of the education, labor market outcomes, and political and civic involvement among second-generation immigrant and native-minority young adults in the New York metropolitan area. Other recent work includes studies of immigrants and politics in New York and Los Angeles, the political incorporation of immigrants in Europe and the U.S. and the comparative study of the second generation in eight European countries. His "Place Matters: A Metropolitics for the 21st Century", co-authored with Peter Dreier and Todd Swanstrom, won the Michael Harrington Prize of the American Political Science Association in 2002. The New York Chapter of the American Planning Association gave him its Robert Ponte award for distinguished contributions to the understanding of economic development in New York City. He received his Ph.D. from Harvard and B.A. from Carleton College.

Demetrios G. Papademetriou (Convenor) is the President of the Migration Policy Institute. He is also the convener of the Transatlantic Council on Migration and its predecessor, the Transatlantic Task Force on Immigration and Integration (co-convened with the Bertelsmann Stiftung). Dr. Papademetriou also convenes the Athens Migration Policy Initiative, a task force of mostly European immigration experts that advises EU Members States on immigration issues. He is the Co-Founder and International Chair Emeritus of "Metropolis: An International Forum for Research and Policy on Migration and Cities". Dr. Papademetriou has been Chair of the Migration Committee of the Organization for Economic Cooperation and Development; Director for Immigration Policy and Research at the US Department of Labor and Chair of the Secretary of Labor's Immigration Policy Task Force; he was also Executive Editor of the *International Migration Review*. Dr. Papademetriou has published more than 200 works (books, articles, monographs, research reports) on migration topics. He advises senior government and political party officials in more than 20 countries.

Gunter Thielen has worked for Bertelsmann since 1980, transforming Bertelsmann's former printing and manufacturing division into Arvato AG, a cutting-edge media- and communications-services provider. In July 2002, the Bertelsmann AG Supervisory Board appointed him chair of the Executive Board. He became chairman and CEO of the Bertelsmann Stiftung in January 2008. Dr. Thielen studied mechanical engineering and economics at Aachen Technical University. After earning a doctorate in engineering, he worked in a variety of executive positions at BASF before becoming technical director of the Wintershall refinery in Kassel. He began his career with Bertelsmann as CEO of the Maul-Belser printing company in Nuremberg. He took over the printing and manufacturing division in 1985, when he also became a member of the Bertelsmann AG executive board. Throughout his years as an executive at the international media company, Dr. Thielen has adhered to the Bertelsmann corporate culture as formulated by the company's founder, Reinhard Mohn. His success has been based on employing the key concepts of decentralization, entrepreneurship and leadership based on partnership.